BY THE EDITORS OF CONSUMER GUIDE®
AND CHARLES MOSHER, M.D.

EMERGENCY FIRST AID

Your knowledge can save lives!

In any emergency the victim needs professional help. At the first opportunity, you must call an ambulance or emergency room.

This publication is *not* to be used *instead* of a doctor, but merely to guide you in helping the victim until the professional arrives. Our guidelines are based on what will happen with *most* victims in most situations; but there are always a few exceptions where the victim may not respond to your first aid as expected. These victims will need professional care even sooner.

So always tell the first person who arrives to assist you to call an ambulance, rescue squad, emergency room, or private doctor, depending on the urgency of the situation. If you are alone, and can do so without endangering the victim, make the call yourself.

Contents

When Seconds Count

Step-by-step instructions and illustrations tell how to handle life-threatening injuries and illnesses.

When Minutes Count

Step-by-step instructions and illustrations tell what to do when faced with emergencies that require treatment but are not likely to be immediately fatal.

Manufactured in the United States of America
1 2 3 4 5 6 7 8 9 10

Library of Congress Cataloging in Publication Data
Main entry under title:
Mosher, Charles.
  Emergency first aid.
  Includes index.
    1. First aid in illness and injury. I. Consumer guide. II. Title.
RC86.7.M67   614.8:8   78-15702
ISBN 0-517-26283-5

This edition published by:

Beekman House
A Division of Crown Publishers, Inc.
One Park Avenue
New York, N.Y. 10016
By arrangement with Publications International, Ltd.

Cover Design: Frank E. Peiler

Illustration: Steven Boswick

Understanding Why You Do What You Do

The medical basis for taking the emergency steps prior to the arrival of professional medical help.

About The Author

Dr. Charles Mosher has worked in emergency rooms in the Los Angeles area, spent two years in South America as a physician with the Peace Corps, and directed the program in Emergency Health for the state of Georgia. He has written several "handbooks" and articles pertaining to medicine and some short stories and poetry. He is presently a country doc in Mariposa, California.

How To Handle Emergencies

THE APPROACH: this publication has been organized pretty much the way you should be organized for a medical emergency. It guides you in a step-by-step manner, according to the most up-to-date approach to emergencies which allows you to be relaxed and helpful to the victim.

The step-by-step method: in an emergency, you should always follow the steps in a certain order. Some of the steps will go faster than others, depending on the specific situation, but the steps are always the same.

The first steps cover things that are an immediate threat to the victim's life. For example:

> blocked airway
> not breathing
> heart not beating

The next steps cover things that could threaten the victim's life a little later if not corrected. For example:

> heavy bleeding
> chest injury

Later steps cover less crucial but still important problems.

The conditions are grouped according to their importance from the medical point of view. Those which are (or could be) an immediate threat to life or eyesight are "Emergencies where every second counts." Conditions that allow you a little more time to work with are called "Emergencies where every minute counts."

Do not panic: you can handle most emergencies quite well by taking time to get organized and going thru the steps outlined here. Common causes of panic in all of us are lots of blood (a cut on the face will bleed heavily, but is rarely fatal), and lots of pain (pain can sometimes point out an emergency situation, but no one ever dies from pain). Do not let such distractions get you out of step.

If you feel like you are panicking, stop — relax — think about the steps — and do them, one by one. Follow each step carefully and completely, then move on.

Common sense and the golden rule: every emergency is a little bit different, even when we are talking about the same injury or illness. For that reason, you may see no need for elaborate examination at certain steps. For instance, if step 1 is "check airway" and the victim is awake and talking, his airway is obviously all right. Or you may need to adapt some steps to the specific situation. Trust your judgment and common sense for this.

But always remember the following Golden Rule:

FIRST, DO NO HARM

If you are unsure what to do to a victim, do not do anything! The last thing you want to do is make the injury worse because you goofed. If you are not sure, leave the care to the professionals or someone else who knows first aid better.

Guidelines and explanations: 21 emergency conditions are included in this publication. Each is discussed twice:

Each condition is outlined in the step-by-step approach in the first part of the book — to be used as a guide when treating the condition. What to do, when and how to do it, and what not to do are included.

In the following pages, each condition is discussed in some detail and an explanation is given for the steps outlined in the step-by-step section. Read the explanatory pages in the latter part of the book to understand the emergency and its treatment.

Homework: there is some information you need to have to make sure you are prepared for an emergency:
1. Call the ambulance service in your town and ask them what the "response time" would be to your house.
2. Do the same with your local rescue squad if you have one (fire department, civil defense, etc.). Find out which station is closest to you.
3. Fill in the blanks for the emergency phone numbers indicated in the step-by-step section.
4. Tape the phone number of the nearest ambulance or rescue squad to all the telephones in your house.

You, the good samaritan: could someone sue you for trying to save his life with first aid? Our judicial system allows anyone to sue for almost anything. That is not the point. The point is, could someone win a suit against you? Not likely.

Some states have "good samaritan" laws that protect first-aiders from such suits. As long as you do your best, do not try to do something you have not been trained for, and do not charge for the service, the "good samaritan" law covers you.

Where there are no such laws, the same rules apply. Do the best you can, do not ask for payment, and do no harm. In such a case, it is unlikely any lawyer would go to court against you, and even less likely a jury would decide against you.

So do not worry about the legal aspects — give good first aid and the law is on your side. At the time of writing this publication, no first-aider had yet been sued to the best of our knowledge.

More help for you: studies indicate that you will be involved in an emergency situation at least twice in your life. Luckily, things have changed drastically in the last few years for the first-aider and the victim.

You are no longer alone. High quality medical care is now available before the victim gets to the hospital in nearly every location in the country. Ambulance attendants and rescue personnel have been trained as Emergency Medical Technicians (EMT's) with hundreds of hours of experience and have saved thousands of lives. So calling for this help will be an important step in most emergencies.

In fact, it is your obligation to call for this help at the very first opportunity. We have indicated under each emergency situation when it is usually safe to leave the victim and call, but remember: the first helper who arrives after you, must be sent immediately to call an ambulance. Or, call yourself as soon as you can leave the victim without endangering him.

Training to teach the basic skills of first aid is now available almost everywhere; the most important training is Cardio-Pulmonary Resuscitation (CPR).

The ideal situation would be for you to go out today (or tomorrow if it is late) and be trained in first aid with lots of practice, and for you to do that every six months to stay sharp, if possible.

There is one absolute must for you, however, you must take a course in CPR. And the sooner you do it the better. This training will teach you the most crucial steps for an emergency and allow you to always be prepared for the worst situation.

CPR A Must

You have finished dinner and you come into the living room to join your husband. You find him on the floor in front of the T.V. You shake him and ask him if he is OK, but his face is pale and he does not respond.

What do you do next?

You are babysitting for a friend's 18 month-old. The baby is in the next room. When you go to check on her, she has a plastic dress cover over her face, is unconscious, and her skin is blue.

What do you do next?

The answer is CPR.

You must take a training course in Cardio-Pulmonary Resuscitation (CPR) so you will be able to help someone who is unconscious and whose heart and/or breathing may have stopped.

> Cardio = heart
> Pulmonary = lung
> Resuscitation = bring back to life

CPR will teach you the first vital steps for helping anyone who is unconscious from any cause.

You must take a training course in CPR because:

1. It is a skill which you can not get by reading. You have to learn it and practice it.
2. It is the only way to keep someone alive when his heart, breathing or both, have stopped.
3. Once you know CPR, most emergencies will be much easier for you to handle, you will already know the first steps to saving a life.

Where can you get a CPR course?

There is hardly a town in the USA that does not have CPR courses going on today. The best thing to do is call your nearest American Heart Association (or American Red Cross) office and ask about courses near you. They should have current information.

In many communities, CPR courses are found in hospitals, fire departments, ambulance services, colleges, YMCA's and other institutions.

But be sure you get the best training available. Do not waste your time with a poorly run program.

How do you recognize a good course?

1. Before you sign up, ask:
   a. How many hours long is the course? It should be at least 6 hours.
   b. How many hours will be spent in manikin practice? It should be at least 2.
   c. Will they also teach you the obstructed airway technique? If not, will they have a course where you can learn it soon?
   d. How many students per instructor? Absolutely no more than 6 (the fewer the better).
   e. If successful, will you get a card from the Heart Association (or Red Cross)? If not, the quality of the course is in doubt.
2. At the end of the course, do you feel competent and comfortable with your knowledge of CPR? If not:
   a. Please tell the instructor. He needs the feedback to improve the course.
   b. Ask the instructor to help you get more practice within the next few days or sign up for another course.

Step 1.

Pinch and shout.

a. Pinch the victim's shoulder.

b. Shout in his ear "Are you OK?" Use his name if you know it.

c. **DO NOT** shake victim violently, especially if it is possible he has a head or neck injury.

Step 2.

If the victim does not respond, yell for help.

Step 3.

Lay the victim on his back on the floor or ground.

a. **DO NOT** let his head strike the ground.

b. **DO NOT** twist or bend the victim's neck.

c. **DO NOT** give him anything to eat or drink.

Step 1: "Are you OK?"

Step 4.

Open the airway.

    a. Lift the neck.

    b. Push back on forehead.

Step 5.

Check for breathing.

    a. Lean over victim's face.

    b. Listen for breathing.

    c. Feel for breathing on your cheek.

    d. Look for chest to rise and fall.

    e. Do this for 5 seconds.

Step 6.

If victim is not breathing, give 4 quick breaths.

    a. Pinch the victim's nose.

    b. Take a deep breath.

    c. Cover victim's mouth with yours.

Step 4: Lift neck and push back on forehead.

Step 5: Look, listen and feel for breath.

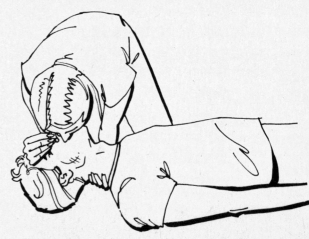

Step 6: Pinch victim's nose and give breaths.

d. Give 4 deep, quick breaths.

e. Take your mouth away after each breath.

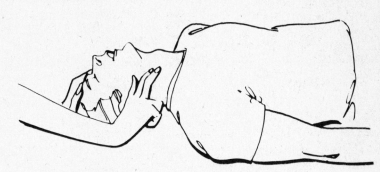

Step 7.

Check the pulse.

Step 7: Gently feel for victim's neck pulse.

a. Keep hand on victim's forehead.

b. Put fingers on Adam's apple.

c. Slide fingers down into neck groove.

d. Gently feel for a neck pulse.

e. Feel for 10 seconds.

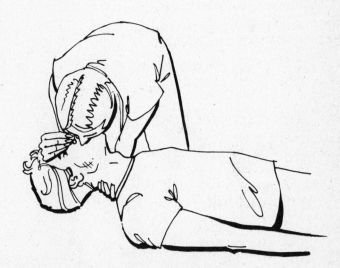

Step 8.

Step 8: Give breath every 5 seconds.

If there is a pulse, give a breath every 5 seconds.

e. Take your mouth off after each breath.

a. Pinch nose.

f. Watch the chest fall.

b. Take deep breath.

g. Repeat every 5 seconds.

c. Cover mouth.

d. Blow forcefully into victim's mouth.

h. Check the pulse from time to time.

Step 9.

Continue breathing until victim breathes on his own or there is no pulse.

Step 10.

If there is no pulse, begin external compressions.

   a. Find the notch at tip of breastbone with middle finger of the hand you used to feel the pulse.

   b. Measure up two finger widths.

   c. Place heel of other hand along lower half of breastbone, above your fingers.

   d. Place your other hand on top.

   e. Straighten your arms.

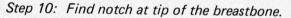

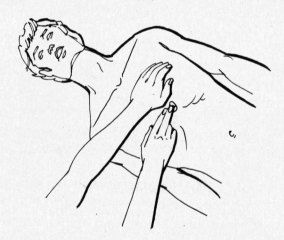

Step 10: Find notch at tip of the breastbone.

Step 10: Place hand along lower half of breastbone.

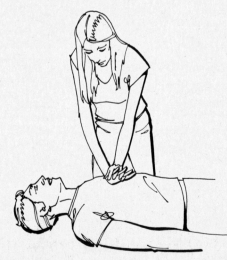

Step 10: Place other hand on top.

f. Press straight down to compress chest 1-1/2 to 2 inches.

g. Each compression lasts 3/4 second.

h. After every 15 compressions, give 2 quick, deep breaths.

Step 11.

Yell for help.

a. If someone else comes, send them to call an ambulance or rescue squad, while you continue compressions and breaths (CPR). Then go to Step 13.

b. If no one else comes, continue CPR for about 5 minutes.

Step 12.

Then call an ambulance or rescue squad.

a. Phone no._____

b. Tell them:

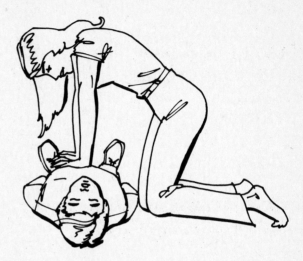

Step 10: Compress chest 1½ to 2 inches.

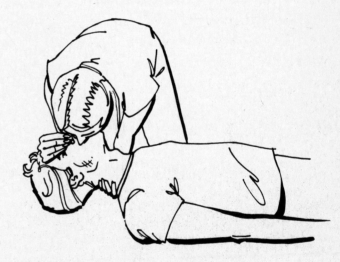

Step 10: 15 compressions and 2 breaths.

Address where you are.

Phone no. where you are.

Victim is unconscious.

CPR is in progress.

Step 13.

Return immediately and continue CPR until:

    a. Victim begins breathing and has a pulse.

    b. Or the ambulance arrives.

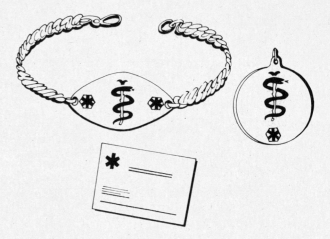

Step 15: Look for medical identification.

Step 14.

If the victim is breathing and there is a pulse, keep airway open.

Step. 15.

Look for medical identification.

    a. Bracelet.

    b. Necklace.

    c. Or wallet card.

Step 16.

If victim is diabetic, give some sugar.

    a. Place under his tongue:

A sugar cube (or)

Granulated sugar, 1/2 tsp. (or)

A piece of candy (or)

A glass of orange juice or soda pop, a few drops at a time.

DO NOT pour juice or other liquids into mouth.

Keep the airway open!

    b. If someone else is there have them call an ambulance. If you are alone, stay with victim giving sugar until you see improvement (about 5 minutes). Then call an ambulance.

Step 17.

If victim is not diabetic, check the skin.

 a. Is the skin red?

 b. Is the skin very hot?

 c. Is the skin dry (even
  underarms)?

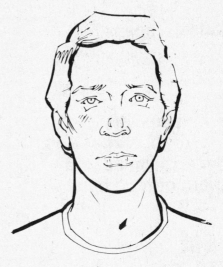

Step 17: Red, hot, dry skin may mean heatstroke.

Step 18.

**If "yes" to these questions,
move victim to cool area.**

**See HEATSTROKE, p. 23,
Steps 4-9.**

Step 19.

**Check breathing and pulse
from time to time.**

Step 19: Look, listen and feel for breath.

Choking Seconds Count

Step 1.

Ask "Can you speak?"

Step 2.

If victim can talk, groan, wheeze, cough, or make any noise like moving air, stay with him and encourage him to cough it out.

> **DO NOT** slap his back or interfere with his efforts.

Step 3.

If victim makes no sound and cannot move air or stops groaning and wheezing, deliver 4 hard back blows.

> a. Stand behind.
>
> b. Hold victim's chest with one hand.
>
> c. Give 4 quick slaps with the palm between the shoulder blades.

Step 4.

Then deliver 4 abdominal thrusts.

> a. Wrap arms around victim's waist.

Step 2: Encourage victim to cough.

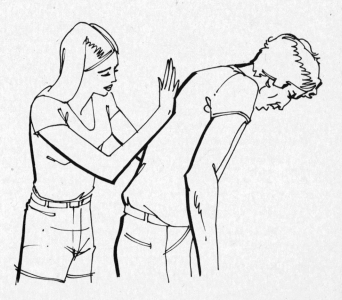

Step 3: If victim makes no sound, give back blows.

b. Find spot between breastbone and navel with one hand.

c. Place thumb side of other fist in that spot, **NOT** over the end of breastbone.

d. Grasp fist with other hand.

Step 4: Find spot between breastbone and navel.

e. Press fist in and upward quickly. Do this 4 times.

Or deliver 4 chest thrusts, if victim is very fat or pregnant:

a. Place arms under victim's armpits and around chest.

Step 4: Press fist in and upward.

b. Place the thumb side of one fist against the breastbone in the middle, not on the lower tip.

c. Grasp fist with other hand.

d. Squeeze the chest quickly with your arms. Do this 4 times.

Step 4: For pregnant woman, give chest thrusts.

Step. 5

Repeat:

4 back blows and
4 abdominal thrusts (or
chest thrusts).

Try to remove object.

Try to give a breath

Step 6.

If the victim becomes
unconscious, carefully lower
him to the floor on his
back.

DO NOT let his head
strike the floor.

Step 7: Open the airway.

Step 7.

Open the airway.

    a. Lift the neck.

    b. Push back on forehead.

Step 8.

Try to give a breath.

a. Pinch the nose.

b. Take a deep breath.

c. Cover his mouth with yours.

d. Blow in forcefully.

e. Watch the chest to see if it rises.

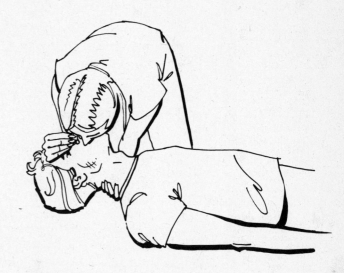

Step 8: Try to give victim a breath.

Step 9.

If the air goes in and the chest rises:

a. Give a breath every 5 seconds.

b. Take your mouth away between breaths.

Step 10.

If no air goes in deliver 4 back blows.

a. Roll victim toward you.

b. Lean him on your thigh.

c. Hold his shoulder.

d. Give 4 slaps with your palm between shoulder blades.

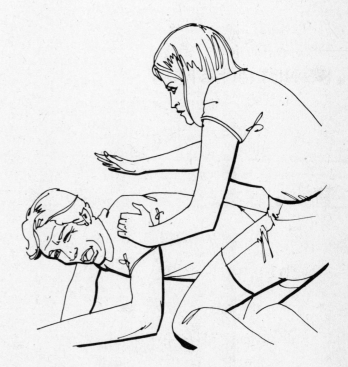

Step 10: If no air goes in, give back blows.

Choking Seconds Count

Step 11.

Roll victim back and give 4 abdominal thrusts.

  a. Place heel of your hand between breastbone and navel.

  b. Place other hand on top.

  c. Press inward and upward quickly. Do this 4 times.

Step 11: Find position for abdominal thrust.

OR

Deliver 4 chest thrusts for pregnant woman.

  a. Place heel of one hand along lower half of breastbone, not on lower tip.

  b. Place other hand on top.

  c. Straighten your arms.

  d. Press straight down quickly to compress chest 1 to 2 inches. Do this 4 times.

Step 11: Deliver chest thrusts to pregnant woman.

Step 12.

Try to remove the blocking object.

     a. Turn head to side.

     b. Lift the jaw and tongue.

     c. Sweep deep in the mouth with index finger in hooked position.

Step 13.

Try to give a breath.

Step 14.

Repeat:
4 back blows and
4 abdominal thrusts (or chest thrusts).
Try to remove object.
Try to give a breath

Until breaths go in, DO NOT leave the victim.

DO NOT begin heart compressions.

DO NOT do any other first aid.

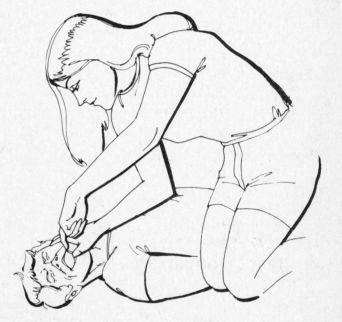

Step 12: Remove blocking object.

Insulin Reaction Seconds Count

Step 1.

Decide: Is the victim diabetic?

    a. Ask victim or family if possible.

    b. Look for medical identification: bracelet, necklace, or a wallet card.

If victim is awake, go to Step 9.

Step 2.

If unconscious, open the airway.

    a. Lift the neck.

    b. Push back on forehead.

Step 3.

Check for breathing.

    a. Lean over victim's face.

    b. Listen for breathing.

    c. Feel for breathing on your cheek.

    d. Look for the chest to rise and fall.

    e. Do this for 5 seconds.

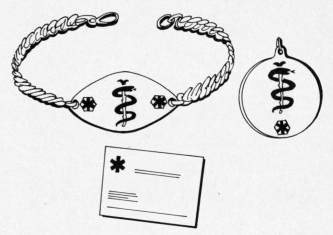
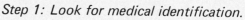

Step 1: Look for medical identification.

Step 2: Lift neck, push back on forehead.

Step 3: Look, listen and feel for breath.

Step 4.

If victim is not breathing, see
UNCONSCIOUSNESS, p. 8,
Steps 6-10.

Step 5.

When breathing and pulse are
all right, place under the
tongue:

    a. A sugar cube, (or)

    b. Granulated sugar, 1/2
        tsp., (or)

    c. A piece of candy (or)

    d. A glass of orange juice
        or soda pop, a few
        drops at a time.

        DO NOT pour juice or
        other liquids into the
        mouth.

        Keep the airway open!

Step 6.

If someone else is there, have
them call an ambulance.

Step 7.

If you are alone, stay with
victim, giving sugar, until you
see improvement (should be
about 5 minutes).

Step 8.

Then call an ambulance.

Step 9.

If victim is awake, give victim
some sugar:

    a. Orange juice (or)

    b. Sugar (or)

    c. Honey (or)

    d. Candy (or)

    e. Soda pop.

Step 10.

Stay with victim until you see
improvement (about 5
minutes).

Step 11.

Call ambulance and return to
victim.

Heatstroke Seconds Count

Step 1.

Decide: Is it heatstroke?

    a. Is the skin red or pale?

    b. Is the skin hot or cool?

    c. Is the skin dry or wet (clammy)?

    d. Is the body temperature high? ("high" is 105 F or more on a thermometer.)

    e. Is the environment warm and humid?

Skin red, hot, and dry = heatstroke.

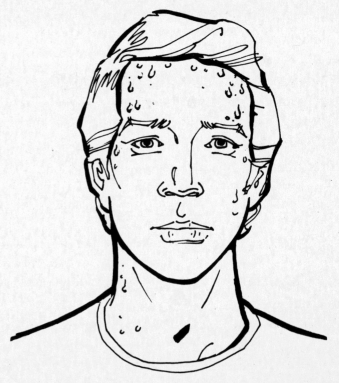

Step 1: Red, hot and dry skin = heatstroke.

Step 2.

DO NOT give victim anything to eat or drink.

Step 3.

Move victim to a cool area (if available right away).

Step 1: Pale, cool and wet skin is not heatstroke.

Step 4.

Remove almost all victim's clothing.

Step 5.

Cover the skin with wet, cold towels or cloths (change them frequently as they get warm).

Step 6.

Fan the victim.

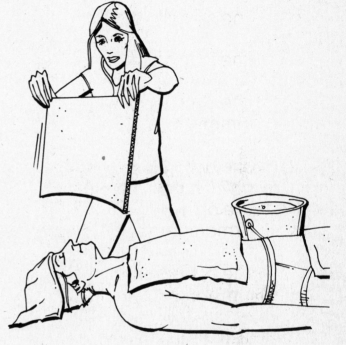

Step 5: Cover the skin with cold, wet towels.

Step 7.

If available, hold victim in a tub of cold water (or a cool pond or stream if there is one). DO NOT use ice. Keep victim's head out of the water!

Step 8.

Check the temperature of victim from time to time.

    a. Feel the skin.

    b. Or use a thermometer.

Step 9.

When temperature is almost normal call the ambulance.

Step 10.

Check breathing and pulse from time to time.

Chemical In Eye Seconds Count

Step 1.

DO NOT let victim rub his eye.

DO NOT let victim keep his eye closed.

Step 2.

Rinse the eye with clean water for 15 minutes (by the clock!). DO NOT use hot water.

a. Have victim lie down near the water (on the floor of bathroom, kitchen, etc.).

b. Hold the eyelids open.

c. Pour water slowly over the eyeball at inner corner.

Step 2: Rinse eye with clean water.

d. Let the water run out of the eye from the outer corner.

Step 3.

If it is your own eye, and you are alone:

    a. Fill bowl or sink with water.

    b. Put your face in water.

    c. Blink your eyes open and closed.

    d. Change the water every 3 to 5 minutes.

Step 3: If you are alone, put your face in water.

Step 4.

DO NOT use antidotes or other chemicals (like vinegar) unless a doctor tells you to.

Step 5.

Take victim to the Emergency Room or doctor's office after the 15 minute rinse.

Auto Accident Minutes Count

Step 1.
Protect yourself.

a. Examine the scene for: fallen electric wires, spilled gas, spilled chemicals, traffic.

b. Remove wires with any long object which cannot conduct electricity: dry wood pole or dry rope.

c. Turn off ignition in wrecked vehicle.

Step 1: Remove any fallen electrical wires.

Step 2.
Quickly look at all the victims.

a. Obviously dead.

b. Obviously all right.

c. Need attention (unconscious, bleeding, others).

First take care of anyone who is unconscious and THEN those who are awake.

d. At first opportunity, send someone to call ambulance.

Step 3.

DO NOT move any victim unless absolutely necessary:

a. In case of fire.

b. Danger of explosion.

c. Danger of drowning.

d. Victim has no pulse.

If victim must be moved: brace head, neck, and back; prevent twisting and bending.

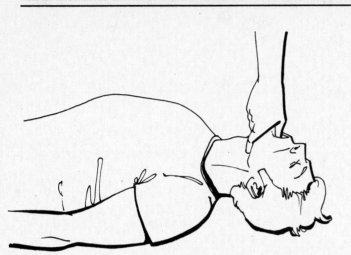

Step 4: Lift jaw and tongue to check airway.

Step 4.

If unconscious:

a. Open airway: Lift jaw and tongue, **DO NOT** bend neck. Clear mouth of blood, teeth, broken bone.

b. Check breathing.

Lean over victim's face.

Listen for breathing.

Feel for breathing on your cheek.

Look for chest to rise and fall.

Do this for 5 seconds.

c. If not breathing see UNCONSCIOUSNESS, p. 8, Steps 6-10.

Remember **DO NOT** bend neck unless absolutely necessary to give breath.

d. Send someone to call an ambulance or if you are alone, after 5 minutes, if pulse and breathing have not returned, call an ambulance. Then quickly return to continue CPR (compressions and breathing).

Step 5.

Look for chest injury.

a. If victim is breathing and has a pulse, take off shirt, blouse, bra and other constrictions.

DO NOT remove any object which is stuck in chest.

b. If chest injury is present, see CHEST INJURY, p. 45, Steps 5-10.

Step 6.

Look for heavy bleeding.

If present see BLEEDING, p. 29, Steps 1-6.

Step 7.

Ask victim if he has neck or back pain.

    a. If so, **DO NOT** move the victim.

    b. Tell victim not to move.

Step 8.

Examine for shock:

    a. Skin pale, cool, clammy.

    b. Victim restless, drowsy.

    c. Victim thirsty.

    d. Pulse rapid (over 100).

Step 9.

If shock is present, see SHOCK, p. 40, Steps 3-9.

Step 10.

If victim complains of neck/back pain or victim is unconscious, support the neck and back. See SPINAL INJURY, p. 49, Steps 3-7.

Step 11.

Call an ambulance.

    a. Dial 911 or Operator.

    b. Give location of accident.

    c. Tell the number of victims.

    d. Return to victim(s) immediately after the call.

Step 12.

Examine for broken bones. If broken bones are present, see BROKEN BONES, p, 75, Steps 4-8.

Step 1.

Apply pressure to the wound.

a. Cover wound with
   bandage:
   Sterile dressing,
   Clean cloth,
   Handkerchief
   Sanitary napkin.

b. Place hand over
   bandage and press
   firmly.

c. Keep pressure on until
   bleeding stops.

d. **DO NOT** remove
   bandages. If soaked
   through, add more
   bandage material and
   keep up the pressure.

Step 1: Apply pressure to the wound.

Step 2.

**Elevate the bleeding part if
possible, unless it is broken.
Get wound higher than heart.**

Step 3.

**Keep victim from moving the
wounded part.**

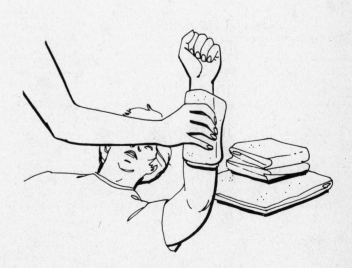

Step 2: Elevate wound above the heart.

Step 4.

DO NOT pour antiseptics on the wound.

Step 5.

If bleeding does not slow down with direct pressure after 5 minutes, push on a pressure point between the wound and body.

Step 5: Pressure points of the body.

a. **Arm wound:** In groove between the big muscles inside upper arm.

Step 5: Pressure point for an arm wound.

b. **Leg wound:** Middle of crease where thigh meets groin.

c. **Neck wound:** In groove to the side of Adam's apple on same side as wound.

Let go of pressure point as soon as bleeding stops.

Step 5: Pressure point for a leg wound.

If signs of shock appear—skin pale, cool, clammy, pulse rapid—and victim is still bleeding, stop the bleeding **immediately,** even with a tourniquet if necessary.

DO NOT wait the 5 minutes indicated.

Step 5: Pressure point for a neck wound.

Bleeding Minutes Count

Step 6.

In case of amputation, or bleeding with shock, use a tourniquet if other methods fail.

a. Use a wide piece of cloth (at least 1-1/2 inches): tie, sock, shirt, sleeve or belt.

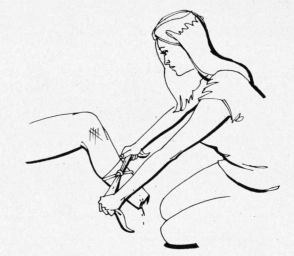

Step 6:   Use a cloth as a tourniquet.

   DO NOT use rope, wire, or string.

b. Place it near (but not touching) wound.

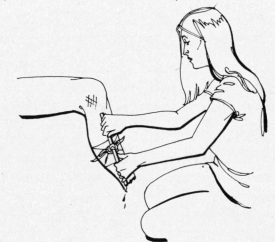

c. Tie a stick to the tourniquet with a single knot.

Step 6:   Tighten the tourniquet with a stick.

d. Twist the stick until bleeding stops but no tighter.

e. Attach the stick to limb to maintain tightness.

Step 6:   Attach the tourniquet to the limb.

f. Write down exact time tourniquet is attached.

g. **DO NOT** remove tourniquet once applied.

A tourniquet is always the last resort, after local pressure and pressure points have been tried.

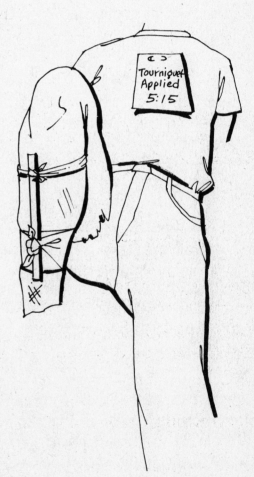

Step 7.

Examine and treat for shock:

a. Skin pale, cool, clammy, victim restless, drowsy. Victim thirsty. Pulse rapid (over 100).

Step 6: Note the time the tourniquet is applied.

b. Stop bleeding immediately by any means necessary.

c. Lay victim down.

d. Prop up legs (about 12 inches). **DO NOT** prop up legs if you suspect a head injury or broken leg.

e. Keep victim warm. Cover with blanket, or jacket.

f. **DO NOT** move victim or let him sit, walk or stand.

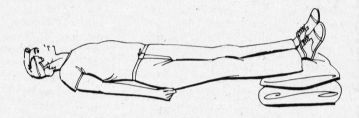

Step 7: Prop up legs.

g. **DO NOT** give victim anything to eat or drink unless there is no medical care available for hours and victim is awake.
Then, mix:

1 quart of water,

1 tsp. salt,

1/2 tsp. baking soda

Give 1/2 glass every 15 minutes. Or give water only if that is all you have.

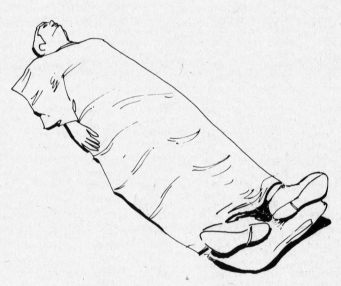

Step 7: Cover the victim with a blanket.

Step 8.

Call ambulance.

Minutes Count Amputation

Step 1.

Apply pressure to the wound.

   a. Cover with bandage:

      Sterile dressing.

      Clean cloth.

      Handkerchief

      Sanitary napkin.

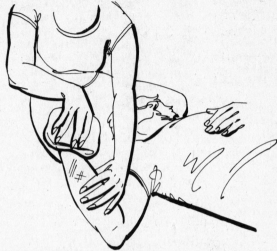

Step 1:   Cover wound and apply pressure.

   b. Press firmly over bandage.

   c. Keep pressure on until bleeding stops.

   d. **DO NOT** remove bandages. If soaked thru, add more bandage material and keep up pressure.

   e. **DO NOT** pour antiseptic on wound.

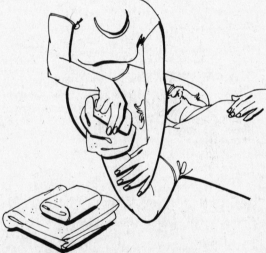

Step 1:   Add more bandage material.

Step 2.

Elevate limb (unless it is broken). Get wound higher than heart.

Step 2:   Elevate the limb above the heart.

Amputation Minutes Count

Step 3.

If bleeding does not slow down after 5 minutes, push on a pressure point between wound and body.

a. **Arm wound:** In groove between the big muscles inside upper arm.

b. **Leg wound:** Middle of crease where thigh meets groin.

Step 3: Pressure points of the body.

Let go of pressure point as soon as bleeding stops.

Step 4.

If signs of shock appear — skin pale, cool, clammy; victim restless, drowsy, thirsty; pulse rapid — and victim is still bleeding, stop the bleeding immediately — even with a tourniquet if necessary.

DO NOT wait the 5 minutes indicated.

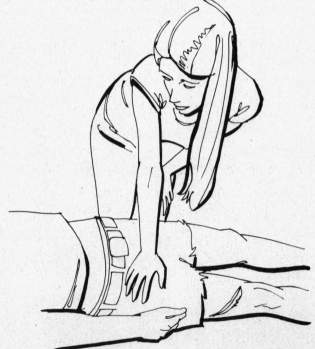

Step 3: Pressure point for leg wound.

Step 5.

If still bleeding after 2 more minutes, or if shock develops, apply a tourniquet.

a. Use a wide piece of cloth (at least 1-1/2 inches): tie, sock, shirt sleeve, or belt.

Step 5: Use a piece of cloth as a tourniquet.

DO NOT use rope, wire, or string.

b. Place it near (but not touching) wound.

c. Tie a stick to the tourniquet with a single knot.

Step 5: Tighten the tourniquet with a stick.

d. Twist the stick until bleeding stops, but no tighter.

e. Attach the stick to limb to maintain tightness.

Step 5: Attach the tourniquet to the limb.

f. Write down time tourniquet is attached.

g. **DO NOT** remove tourniquet once it is applied.

Step 6.

Examine and treat for shock.

a. Skin pale, cool, clammy. Victim restless, drowsy. Victim thirsty. Pulse rapid (over 100).

b. Stop bleeding by any means necessary.

c. Lay victim down.

d. Prop up legs (about 12 inches).

   DO NOT prop up legs if you suspect a head injury or broken leg.

e. Keep victim warm. Cover with blanket or jacket.

f. **DO NOT** let victim sit, walk, or stand.

Step 5: Note the time the tourniquet is applied.

Step 6: Prop up the legs about 12 inches.

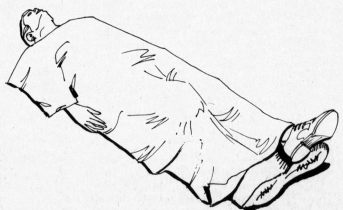

Step 6: Cover the victim with a blanket.

g. **DO NOT** give anything to eat or drink, unless there is no medical care available for hours, and victim is awake. Then, mix:

1 quart water

1 tsp. salt

1/2 tsp. baking soda

Give 1/2 glass every 15 minutes or give water if that is all you have.

Step 7.

Call ambulance

Phone no. _____

Step 8.

Wrap the amputated part in a clean cloth, place in plastic bag, and pack in ice.

DO NOT put the part in water, alcohol, or antiseptic.

Step 9.

Give part to ambulance attendants.

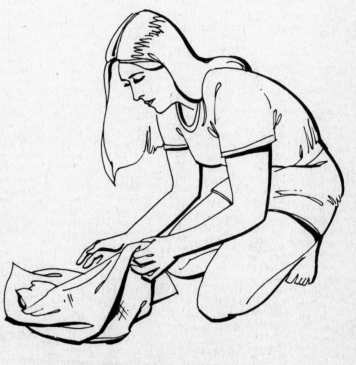

Step 8: Wrap the amputated part in clean cloth.

Shock Minutes Count

Step 1.

Examine for shock.

   a. Skin pale.

   b. Skin clammy (cool and sweating).

   c. Victim restless or drowsy.

   d. Victim thirsty.

   e. Obvious bleeding or possible internal bleeding (from auto accident, fall, etc.).

   f. Pulse rapid (over 100).

   g. Breathing rapid and weak.

   h. Pupils are large.

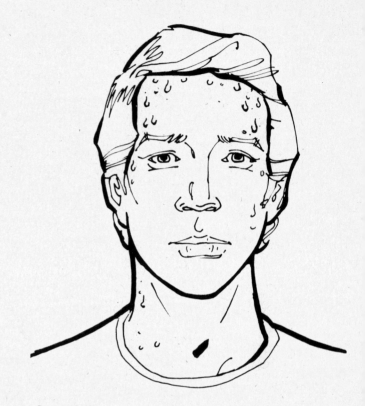

Step 1: Pale and clammy skin may indicate shock.

Step 2.

If many of these signs are present or if you suspect shock, lay victim down.

DO NOT let victim sit, walk, or stand.

Step 3.

Prop up victim's legs (about 12 inches).

DO NOT prop up legs if you suspect a head injury or broken leg.

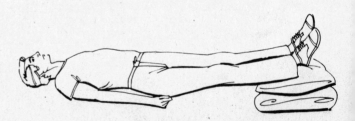

Step 3: Prop up legs about 12 inches.

Step 4.

Stop bleeding.

   a. Cover wound with bandage:

      Sterile dressing.

      Clean cloth.

      Handkerchief.

      Sanitary napkin.

Step 4: Cover wound with clean cloth and press.

   b. Place hand over bandage and press firmly.

   c. If bleeding does not slow almost immediately, push on a pressure point between wound and body.

Step 4: Pressure points in the body.

Arm wound: In groove between the big muscles inside upper arm.

Leg wound: Middle of crease where thigh meets groin.

Neck wound: In groove to the side of Adam's apple on same side as wound.

Step 4: Pressure point for arm wound.

d. Let go of pressure point after the bleeding stops, but push it again if bleeding starts again.

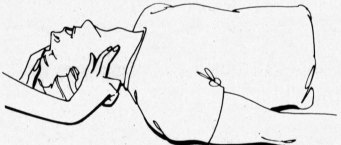

Step 4: Pressure point for neck wound.

e. In case of amputation, or if other methods fail within 2 to 3 minutes, use a tourniquet. See AMPUTATION, p. 37, Step 5.

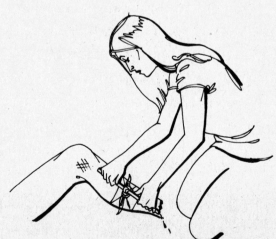

Step 4: In case of amputation, use a tourniquet.

Step 5.

Keep victim warm. Cover with a blanket, jacket.

Step 6.

Call ambulance.

Step 7.

DO NOT move victim unless absolutely necessary.

Step 8.

DO NOT give victim alcohol.

Step 9.

DO NOT give victim anything to eat or drink.

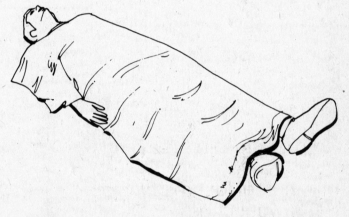

Step 5: Cover victim with a blanket or jacket.

Unless there is no medical care available for hours and the victim is awake. Then, mix:

1 quart water,

1 tsp. salt,

1/2 tsp. baking soda,

Give 1/2 glass every 15 minutes. Or give water only if that is all you have.

Chest Injury Minutes Count

Step 1.
Check the airway.

a. If unconscious, lift neck and push back on forehead. Unless you suspect neck injury, see Spinal Injury p. 49, Step 2.

b. Clear mouth of blood, teeth, broken bone.

Step 1: Lift neck and push back on forehead.

Step 2.
Check for breathing.

a. Lean over victim's face.

b. Listen for breathing.

c. Feel for breathing on your cheek.

d. Look for chest to rise and fall.

e. Do this for 5 seconds.

Step 2: Look, listen and feel for breathing.

Step 3.
If not breathing, give breaths.

a. Pinch nose.

b. Take a deep breath.

c. Cover victim's mouth with yours.

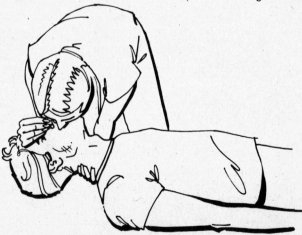

Step 3: Pinch nose and give breaths.

d. Give 4 deep, quick breaths.

e. Take mouth away after each breath.

f. Give one breath every 5 seconds.

Step 4.

If victim is breathing and has a pulse, take off shirt, blouse, bra, other constrictions.

DO NOT remove any object which is stuck in chest.

Step 5.

Examine chest (compare both sides, front and back).

Step 6.

Is the skin pale or blue and is victim gasping for breath?

a. Rush victim to hospital immediately, by car if ambulance is not available.

b. Keep the airway open.

c. Check breathing frequently.

d. Be prepared to give artificial breaths.

Step 7.

Is there a hole or a sucking noise?

a. Cover hole with hand.

b. Then cover with:

Sterile pads.

Plastic bag.

Tin foil.

Anything that will not let air thru.

c. Tape in place. Or hold on with victim's arm or hand.

d. Keep victim in most comfortable position.

e. If victim rapidly gets worse, try lifting the cover to let out built-up pressure. But cover the hole again each time victim breathes in.

Step 8.

Does part of one side move differently from the whole chest? (A bulge when victim breathes out).

Step 8: Lay victim down on bulging chest.

a. Hold the bulging part with your hand so it does not bulge when victim breathes out.

b. Tape a pillow or folded towel over the bulging part.

c. Or have victim lie down with bulging part down.

d. Or have victim hold pillow or towel over bulging part.

Step 8: Have victim hold pillow to bulging chest.

Step 9.

Is there something stuck in the chest (like a knife or screwdriver)?

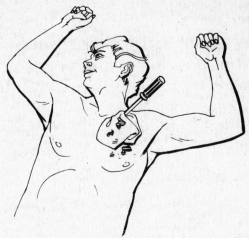

a. **DO NOT** remove it!

b. Carefully wrap a cloth around it if there is a sucking noise coming from that area.

Step 9: Wrap a cloth around object in chest.

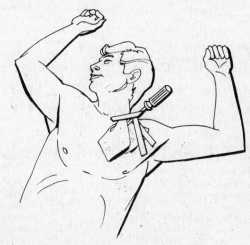

c. If possible, tape the object to the chest without moving it.

Step 10.

Step 9: Tape the object to the chest.

Is there bleeding from the chest?

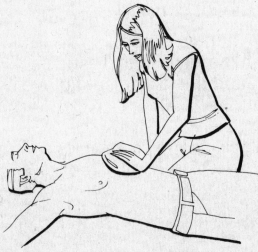

a. Cover spot with a bandage, clean cloth, or handkerchief, and press with your hand.

b. Treat for shock, see p. 40, Steps 3-9.

Step 10: Apply pressure to a bleeding wound.

Chest Injury Minutes Count

Step 11.

Is there pain in the chest, but no other problem with the chest?

    a. Feel gently along the ribs near the pain.

    b. If the pain is worse at a certain point when you press on the rib, it is probably a broken rib.

    c. Wrap a cloth or tape around the chest, over the break, tight enough to ease pain, but not so tight that victim cannot breath easily. Use victim's arm to protect painful spot.

    d. Call ambulance.

Step 12.

Examine for shock:

    a. Skin pale, cool, clammy, victim restless, and thirsty, pulse rapid (over 100).

    b. If shock is present, see SHOCK, p. 40, Steps 3-9.

Step 13.

Call ambulance.

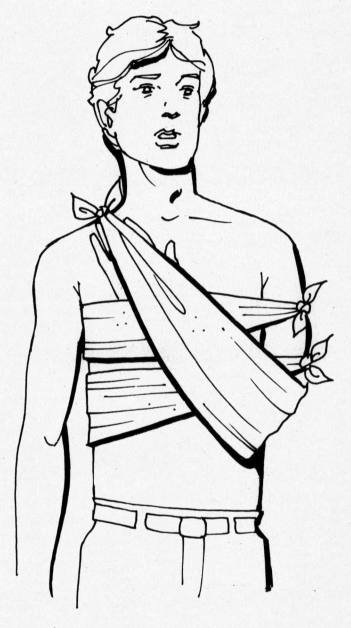

Step 11: Wrap a broken rib.

Step 1.

Decide — is spinal injury possible?

a. Victim unconscious and in an accident.

b. Victim unconscious with bruises or cuts on head.

c. Victim awake but not moving.

d. Victim has pain in neck or back.

In all these cases and whenever it seems like a neck or back injury is possible, treat the victim for spinal injury.

Step 2.

Check the airway.

a. **DO NOT** bend the neck.

b. Look, listen, and feel for breathing.

c. If victim has trouble breathing:
Lift the jaw and tongue.

Or

Place fingers at angles of jaw and pull jaw forward.

DO NOT move neck at all unless absolutely necessary to open the airway.

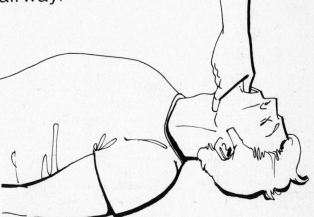

Step 2: Lift the jaw and tongue to check airway.

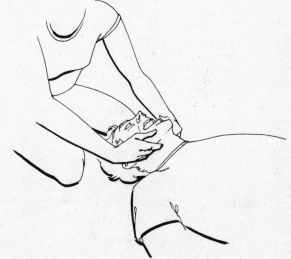

Step 2: Pull jaw forward without moving neck.

Step 3.

DO NOT move victim unless his life is in danger:

a. In case of fire.

b. Danger of explosion.

c. Danger of drowning.

d. Victim has no pulse.

Step 4.

If victim must be moved, try to keep his head, neck, and back straight and well supported.

Step 5.

If victim is awake, tell him to stay still.

Step 6.

If victim is lying down, support his spine so it will not move.

a. **DO NOT** put a pillow under his head.

b. Use rocks, rolled-up clothes, blankets, at side of head, or hold neck and head in position you found them.

c. Call ambulance.

Step 7.

If victim is sitting, support his head so it will not move.

a. Get behind victim.

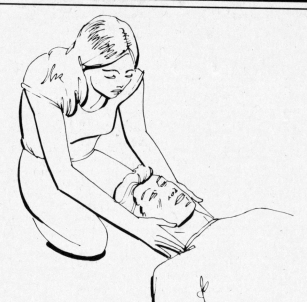

Step 6: Hold the victim's head in position.

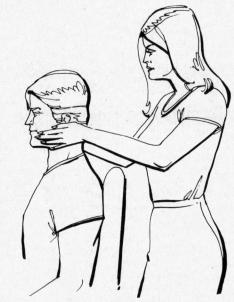

Step 7: If victim is sitting, support his head.

b. Place hands on sides of victim's head and hold steady.

c. Tell next person who arrives to call ambulance.

Step 1.

Decide — is head injury possible?

a. Victim unconscious and in an accident.

b. Victim unconscious with bruises or cuts on head.

c. Victim confused or drowsy and in an accident.

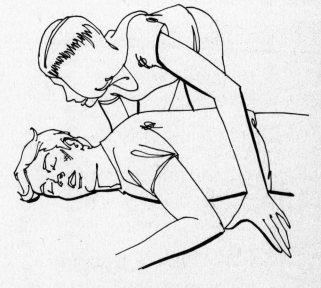

d. Clear fluid draining from nose or ear.

Step 1: Decide if head injury is possible.

e. Victim was unconscious.

In all these cases and whenever it seems like a head injury is possible, treat the victim for head injury.

Step 2.

Check the airway.

a. **DO NOT** bend the neck.

b. Look, listen, feel for breathing.

c. If victim has trouble breathing:

Lift the jaw and tongue.

Or

Place fingers at angle of jaw and pull jaw forward.

DO NOT move neck at all unless absolutely necessary to open the airway.

d. Clear blood, teeth, pieces of bone from mouth.

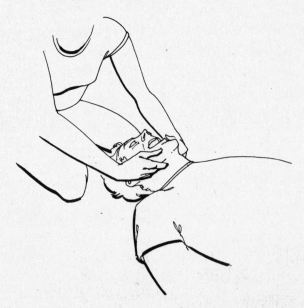

Step 2: Lift jaw and tongue to open airway.

Step 2: Pull jaw forward without moving neck.

Step 3.

Stop bleeding.

    a. Cover wound with
      bandage:

      Sterile dressing.

      Clean cloth.

      Handkerchief.

      Sanitary napkin.

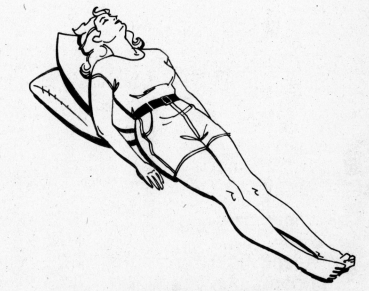

    b. Place hand over
      bandage and hold snug.

Step 4: Keep head elevated and neck straight.

    c. **DO NOT** press hard
      where the skull might
      be broken.

Step 4.

**Keep head elevated when lying
down and keep neck straight.**

Step 5.

Cover open wounds in head with:

    a. Sterile dressing,

    b. Clean cloth,

    c. Handkerchief,

    d. Sanitary napkin.

Step 5: Cover open wound with bandage.

Step 6.

Call ambulance.

> If victim has been unconscious, even for just a few seconds but is now awake, he must get to an emergency room.

Step 8.

DO NOT give victim anything to eat or drink.

Step 9.

DO NOT give victim any medicine.

Step 7.

Keep airway open.

If victim is awake, go to Step 11.

Step 1.

If victim is unconscious lay the victim on his back on the floor or ground.

Step 2.

Open the airway.

    a. Lift the neck.

    b. Push back on forehead.

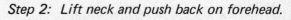

Step 2: Lift neck and push back on forehead.

Step 3.

Check for breathing.

    a. Lean over victim's face.

    b. Listen for breathing.

    c. Feel for breathing on your cheek.

    d. Look for chest to rise and fall.

    e. Do this for 5 seconds.

Step 3: Look, listen and feel for breath.

Step 4.

If not breathing, give breaths.

a. Pinch the nose.

b. Take a deep breath.

c. Cover victim's mouth with yours.

d. Give 4 deep, quick breaths.

e. Take your mouth away after each breath.

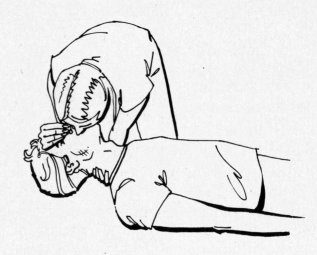

Step 4: Pinch nose and give breaths.

Step 5.

Check the pulse.

a. Put fingers on Adam's apple.

b. Slide fingers down into neck groove.

c. Gently feel for a neck pulse.

d. Feel for 10 seconds.

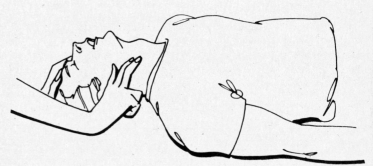

Step 5: Gently feel for a neck pulse.

Step 6.

If there is a pulse, give breaths.

a. Give 1 breath every 5 seconds.

b. Check pulse from time to time.

Step 7.

If there is no pulse, begin external compressions.

a. Find notch at tip of breastbone.

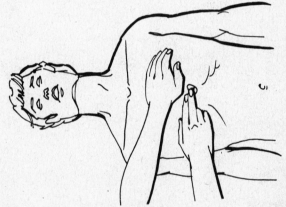

Step 7: Find notch at tip of breastbone.

b. Measure up two fingers.

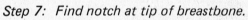

Step 7: Place hand along lower half of breastbone.

c. Place heel of other hand along lower half of breastbone, **NOT** on tip.

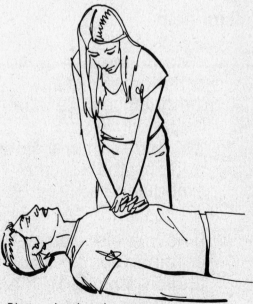

d. Place other hand on top.

e. Straighten your arms.

Step 7: Place other hand on top.

f. Press straight down to compress chest 1-1/2 to 2 inches.

g. Each compression lasts 3/4 second.

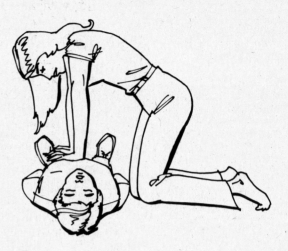

Step 7: Compress chest 1½ to 2 inches.

h. After every 15 compressions, give 2 quick, deep breaths.

Step 8.

Yell for help.

a. If someone else comes, tell them to call an ambulance or rescue squad while you continue compressions and breaths until the ambulance arrives.

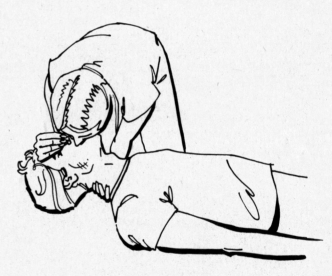

Step 7: After 15 compressions, give 2 breaths.

Step 9.

Then call an ambulance or rescue squad.

a. Phone no. _____

b. If no one else comes, continue compressions and breaths (CPR) for about 5 minutes.

b. Tell them:

Address where you are.

Phone number where you are.

CPR is in progress.

Step 10.

Return immediately to victim and continue CPR.

Step 11.

If victim is awake, call an ambulance or rescue squad.

a. Ambulance phone no._____

b. Rescue squad phone no._____

c. Tell them:

Address where you are.

Phone number where you are.

This is a possible heart attack.

Victim is awake.

Step 12.

Put victim in the most comfortable position. DO NOT force him to lie down.

Step 13.

Let victim take nitroglycerine pills as prescribed.

Step 14.

Stay with the victim.

a. Watch for sudden unconsciousness and disappearance of breathing and pulse.

b. Be prepared to give artificial breaths and compressions.

Step 15.

DO NOT take victim to hospital yourself unless no ambulance is available.

Step 16.

DO NOT let victim refuse to go to hospital.

Drowning Minutes Count

Step 1.

Protect yourself.

a. Throw a life preserver, rope, inner tube.

b. Reach with a pole.

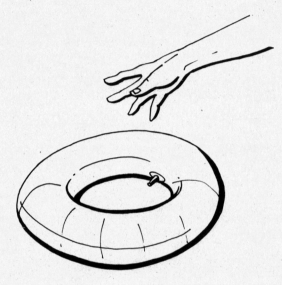

Step 1: Throw a life preserver to the victim.

c. Row out in boat.

d. Swim to victim as last resort.

Step 2.

If victim is not breathing give breaths in water if possible.

a. Turn victim's face up.

b. Keep neck straight while turning.

c. Pinch nose.

d. Take a deep breath.

e. Cover victim's mouth with yours.

f. Blow forcefully into victim's mouth.

g. Give 1 breath every 5 seconds.

Step 3.

Bring victim to shore or edge of pool.

Step 4.

Ask yourself — is a neck injury possible?

a. Diving accident.

b. Surfing accident.

Step 2 : Turn the victim face up.

Step 2: Give the victim a breath in the water.

Step 3: Bring the victim to shore.

Step 5.

If neck injury is possible, keep neck from twisting or bending.

a. Continue breaths if necessary.

b. Call for help.

c. With help:

Place board under victim (surfboard, long piece of wood, etc.).

Gently raise board until it supports victim's whole body.

Remove victim (on board) to land.

d. Keep giving breaths.

e. Do not bend neck.

Step 5: Carry victim with neck injury to shore.

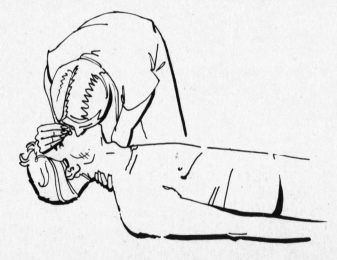

Step 5: Continue to give victim breaths.

Step 6.

Check pulse.

   a. Keep hand on victim's forehead.

   b. Put fingers on Adam's apple.

   c. Slide fingers down into neck groove.

   d. Gently feel for a neck pulse.

   e. Feel for 10 seconds.

Step 6: Gently feel for victim's neck pulse.

Step 7.

If there is a pulse, give a breath every 5 seconds.

   a. Pinch nose.

   b. Take deep breath.

   c. Cover mouth.

   d. Blow forcefully into victim's mouth.

   e. Take your mouth off after each breath.

   f. Watch the chest fall.

   g. Repeat every 5 seconds.

Step 7: Watch victim's chest rise and fall.

Drowning Minutes Count

Step 8.

If there is no pulse, begin external compressions, see UNCONSCIOUSNESS p. 8, Step 10.

Step 9.

If victim vomits:

    a. Quickly turn head to side, or turn whole body to side if you suspect neck injury, supporting the head.

    b. Clean out mouth.

    c. Quickly continue compressions and breaths.

Step 9: Turn victim's head if he vomits.

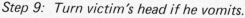

Step 10.

When victim recovers, cover with a blanket, jacket, towels.

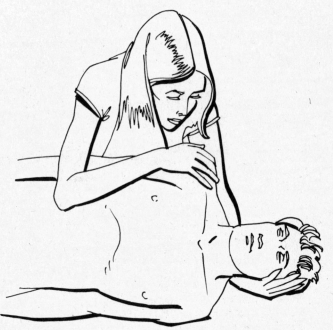

Step 9: If neck injury, turn the whole body.

Step 11.

Call ambulance.

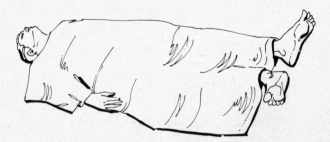

Step 10: Cover the victim with a blanket.

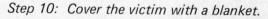

If victim is awake, go to Step 6.

Step 1.

If victim is unconscious, open the airway.

    a. Lift the neck.

    b. Push back on forehead.

Step 1: Lift neck and push back on forehead.

Step 2.

Check for breathing.

    a. Lean over victim's face.

    b. Listen for breathing.

    c. Feel for breathing on your cheek.

    d. Look for chest to rise and fall.

    e. Do this for 5 seconds.

Step 2: Look, listen and feel for breath.

Drug Overdose Minutes Count

Step 3.

If not breathing, give breaths.

    a. Pinch the nose.

    b. Take a deep breath.

    c. Cover victim's mouth with yours.

    d. Give 4 deep, quick breaths.

    e. Take your mouth away after each breath.

    f. Give 1 breath every 5 seconds.

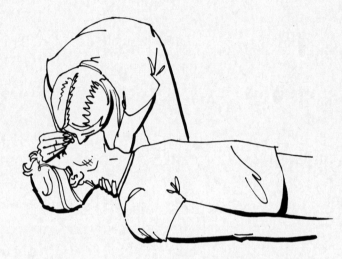

Step 3: Pinch nose and give 4 quick breaths.

Step 4.

If victim is breathing:

    a. Lay victim on side.

    b. Keep airway open.

Step 5.

If victim vomits:

    a. Quickly turn head to side.

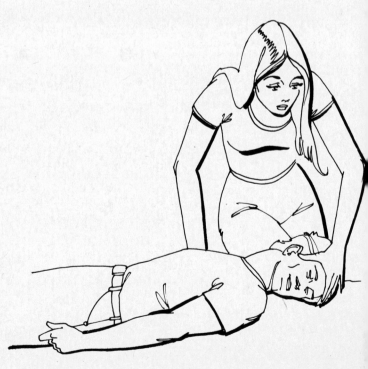

Step 5: If victim vomits, quickly turn his head.

b. Clean out mouth afterward.

c. Check for breathing.

Step 6.

If awake, make victim vomit.

a. Give syrup of ipecac (dose on label).

b. Make victim drink several glasses of water after the ipecac.

c. Or tickle back of throat with finger.

d. **DO NOT** use salt solutions.

Step 6: Use syrup of ipecac to make victim vomit.

Step 7.

Call ambulance.

a. Phone no._____

b. Or take victim to nearest Emergency Room.

Step 8.

Take the drug or pills or empty bottle with you to the hospital.

Step 8: Take drug or empty bottle to hospital.

Poison Swallowed Minutes Count

Step 1.

Be calm — less than 20% of suspected poisonings need hospital treatment.

Step 2.

Look for the medicine, liquid, poison swallowed or its container.

Step 3.

Call the nearest Emergency Room or Poison Control Center.

    a. Emergency Room
       phone no. _____

    b. Poison Control Center
       phone no._____

Step 4.

Tell them:

    a. Name and ingredients
       of the poison from the
       label.

    b. How much you think
       was swallowed.

Step 5.

Follow their instructions.

Step 6.

If you go to the hospital, take the poison bottle.

Step 7.

DO NOT give antidotes.
DO NOT induct vomiting unless directed to by Emergency Room or Poison Control Center.

Step 8.

DO NOT give salt solution.

Step 4: Check label for ingredients.

Step 1.

Carefully ease victim to floor or ground.

Step 2.

Hold victim firmly, but gently.

    a. **DO NOT** let victim's head strike the ground.

    b. **DO NOT** let victim hurt himself.

Step 3.

Try to separate victim's teeth.

Step 3: Separate victim's teeth with a wallet.

    a. Use the corner of your wallet or corner of a paperback book.

    b. **DO NOT** put your finger in victim's mouth.

    c. **DO NOT** use force to separate victim's teeth.

    d. If this is difficult to do. **DO NOT** do it.

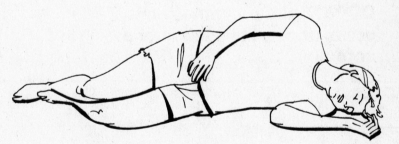

Step 5: Lay the victim on his side.

Step 4.

Stay with the victim until seizure is over.

Step 5.

Lay victim on his side.

Step 6.

Open the airway.

    a. Lift the neck

    b. Push back on forehead.

    c. Check for easy
       breathing.

Step 7.

Call ambulance.

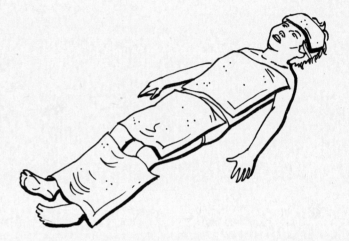

Step 10: Put cold, wet towels on victim.

Step 8.

**DO NOT allow victim to walk,
drive, or exert himself after a
convulsion.**

Step 9.

**DO NOT give victim anything
to eat or drink.**

Step 10.

If victim is a child with a fever:

    a. Give aspirin.

    b. Remove clothes.

    c. Put cold, wet towels on
       victim's body until fever
       is down.

    d. Call ambulance.

Step 1.

Lay victim on his back on floor or ground.

Step 2.

Open the airway.

    a. Lift the neck.

    b. Push back on forehead.

Step 2: Lift neck, push back on forehead.

Step 3.

Check for breathing.

    a. Lean over victim's face.

    b. Listen for breathing.

    c. Feel for breathing on your cheek.

    d. Look for the chest to rise and fall.

    e. Do this for 5 seconds.

If victim is breathing, go to Step 8.

Step 3: Look, listen and feel for breath.

Step 4.

If not breathing, see UNCONSCIOUSNESS, p. 8, Steps 6-10.

Step 5.

Send someone to call ambulance or, if you are alone, continue compressions and breaths (CPR) for about 5 minutes.

Step 6.

Then call an ambulance.

    a. Phone no. _____

    b. Tell the address where you are.

    c. Tell the phone number where you are.

Step 7.

Return to victim immediately and continue CPR.

Step 8.

If victim is breathing and there is a pulse, lay victim on his side.

Step 8: If victim is breathing, lay him on side.

Step 9.

Tell the victim you are going to call for help and you will be right back. Be careful what you say! The victim can probably still hear very well.

Step 10.

DO NOT give victim anything to eat or drink.

Step 1.

Wash your hands.

Step 2.

Rinse the eye with clean water for about 5 minutes.

DO NOT use hot water.

a. Have victim lie down.

b. Hold the eyelids open.

c. Pour water slowly over the eyeball at inner corner.

d. Let the water run out of the eye from outer corner.

Step 2: Rinse eye with clean water for 5 minutes.

Step 3.

If it is your own eye and you are alone:

a. Fill bowl or sink with water.

b. Put your face in water.

c. Blink your eye open and closed.

d. Move your eyes in all directions.

Step 3: If you are alone, put your face in water.

Step 4.

Go to an Emergency Room or doctor's office.

Step 1.

Check the airway.

  a. If unconscious, lift jaw and tongue. **DO NOT** bend neck.

  b. Clear mouth of blood, teeth, broken bone.

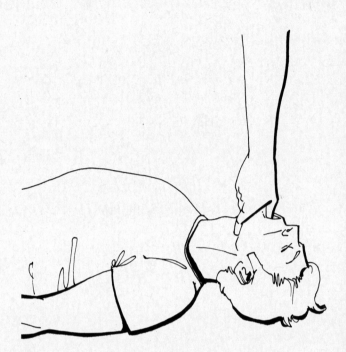

Step 1: Lift jaw and tongue to check airway.

Step 2.

Control heavy bleeding.

  a. Cover with sterile bandage, clean cloth, handkerchief, sanitary napkin.

  b. Press until bleeding stops.

  c. Be careful not to cause movement or pain.

Step 3.

Examine for shock.

  a. Skin pale, cool, clammy, victim restless, and thirsty, pulse rapid (over 100).

  b. If shock present, see SHOCK, p. 40, Steps 2-9.

Step 4.

Examine the injury.

   a. Is it OPEN (a wound near the break), or CLOSED (no break in the skin)?

   b. Cover open breaks with bandage, clean cloth, sanitary napkin. **DO NOT** try to clean up wound.

   c. Check the pulse and skin color on the limb away from the break.

   d. Check if the victim can feel you touch the skin away from the break.

Step 5.

Immobilize the broken bone.

   a. Rule 1: Fix the joint above and the joint below the break so they cannot move.

   b. Rule 2: **DO NOT** move broken bone to put on splint. **DO NOT** try to straighten bent arms or legs.

   c. Use any splint method that works:

      Pillows
      Blankets
      Boards
      Magazines
      Newspapers
      Cardboard
      Baseball bat
      Umbrella
      Belt
      Tie
      Normal toe, leg
      Hold it with arm

   d. **Fingers:** Splint with a stick.

Step 5: Splint finger with a stick.

e. **Hand, wrist, forearm:**
Splint both sides of
forearm from elbow to
wrist. Then, use a sling
(thumb points up; fingers
higher than elbow).

f. **Upper arm, collarbone,
shoulder, elbow broken
and bent:** Use a sling.
Tie the sling to the
chest, or have victim
hold it.

Step 5: Splint forearm from elbow to wrist.

Step 5: For upper arm injury, tie sling to chest.

Step 5: Use a sling so thumb points up.

g. **Elbow broken and straight:** Use a long splint from armpit past wrist.

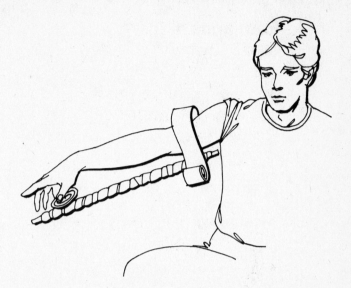

Step 5: For elbow injury, use a long splint.

h. **Pelvis:** Keep victim still. Tie legs together. Examine and treat for shock. **DO NOT** move victim unless absolutely necessary.

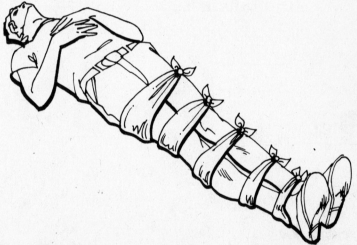

Step 5: For leg or pelvis injury, tie legs together.

i. **Leg:** Place padding between legs. Tie legs together.

j. **Knee broken and bent:** Use a firm splint between upper and lower leg.

Step 5: For a knee injury, use a firm splint.

k. **Foot and ankle:**
Carefully remove shoe, cut off if necessary. Tie on thick, soft splint like a pillow or blanket. Raise the foot.

Step 6.

Call an ambulance.

Phone no._____

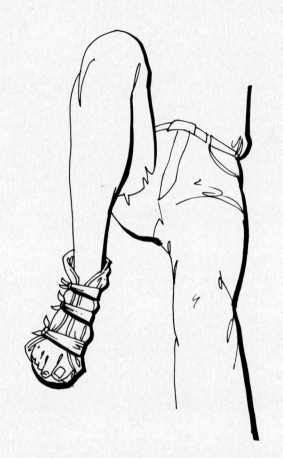

Step 5: For a foot injury, use a thick, soft splint.

Step 7.

Check the splinted part from time to time for:

a. Increased pain.

b. Decreased feeling on skin.

c. Lack of pulse.

d. Pale or blue skin color.

Step 8.

If any of these occur, check the splint for:

a. Ties that are too tight.

b. Unbroken joint that is bent too much.

c. Correct the problem.

Step 1.

Decide what degree of burn victim has:

   a. Is burn red and painful (like sunburn)? Treat as first degree.

   b. Is burn red, painful, with blisters? Treat as second degree.

   c. Is burn black, painless, or white? Treat as third degree.

Step 2.

If first degree only:

   a. Put burned part in cold water.
   DO NOT put ice or salt in water.

   b. Put cold water bottle on burn.

Step 3.

If second degree only:

   a. Put burned part in cold water.
   DO NOT put ice or salt in water.

   b. Put ice cold, wet dressings on burn. Use clean, freshly ironed cloths if available.

   c. Call doctor. If not available, call Emergency Room.

   d. **DO NOT** break blisters.

   e. **DO NOT** put on butter or ointments.

   f. **DO NOT** remove skin.

Step 2: Submerge first degree burn in cold water.

Step 4.

If third degree:

a. Leave burned clothes on the skin.

b. If face is burned, keep victim sitting up.

c. Keep airway open, tilt head back.

d. Call ambulance.

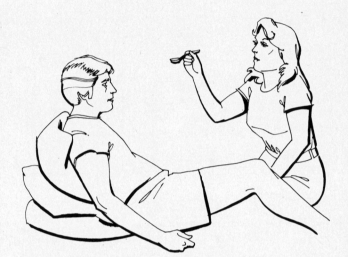

Step 4: Give victim salt water solution.

e. If no medical care is available for over an hour and victim is awake, mix:

1 quart water,

1 tsp. salt,

1/2 tsp. baking soda.

Give 1/2 glass every 15 minutes, or give water only if that is all you have.

f. Elevate burned arms, legs, hands. Keep burn higher than heart.

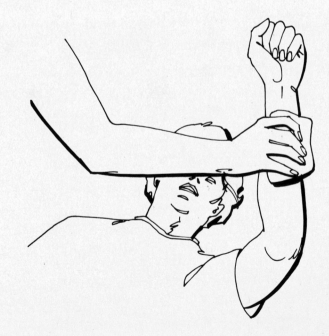

Step 4: Keep burn higher than heart.

Seconds Count

Unconsciousness

There are many different causes for unconsciousness, but only a few possible causes of rapid death that first aid can do anything about:

1. Not enough oxygen for the brain.
2. Very low blood sugar level which injures the brain.
3. Very high temperature which injures the brain.

YOUR GOAL IS:

TO KEEP THE BRAIN ALIVE, UNDAMAGED.

The "Pinch and Shout" is done to be sure the victim is truly unconscious and not just sleeping, drunk, or fainted. You do not start CPR on someone who is breathing or whose heart is beating, it could be dangerous.

If the victim may have had an accident, however, do not move their shoulder or neck— movements could worsen the back or neck injury.

If the victim does not respond and therefore is unconscious, remember that the brain needs oxygen to stay alive and undamaged.

The first requirement is for oxygen to have a pathway into the body, *i.e.*, **airway**. This is always the first concern in **any** emergency. You must open the airway immediately because:

a. The tongue will frequently fall back in the throat and block the airway in an unconscious victim. This is because the muscles are relaxed.

b. You cannot tell if the victim is breathing or not until the airway is open.

The second requirement is for oxygen to get into the lungs *i.e.*, **breathing**. Examine the victim for breathing—if there is none, you provide life-giving oxygen by the mouth-to-mouth technique. Arm moving and chest squeezing methods are not often used anymore. Sometimes an unconscious victim will have a stoma (a breathing hole in the neck) in which case you breathe into his stoma, not his mouth. The air you exhale still is 16% oxygen, and this is enough to save a life.

The third requirement is for blood to pick up oxygen from the lungs and carry it to the brain, *i.e.*, **circulation** (pulse). Feel for the neck (carotid) pulse for ten seconds by the clock before you decide there is no heartbeat. If you think there might be a pulse, or if you are not sure, do not compress the chest. That could injure the victim more. Just keep breathing for the victim and check the pulse frequently.

When you give external compressions, the heart gets squeezed between the breastbone and the spine. The heart valves ensure that the blood flows forward and not backward.

If you do CPR (cardiopulmonary resuscitation) well, enough oxygen will reach the brain to keep it alive until the ambulance arrives. But remember that even the very best CPR is only about 30% as effective as a normal heartbeat, so do not be sloppy or the brain will get even less than 30% of its normal oxygen supply.

If breathing and pulse are normal, then the brain's next enemy might be a very low blood sugar—almost always caused by an over-reaction to insulin injected by a diabetic.

Some sugar in the blood immediately could save such a diabetic's life. If the person is totally unconscious, put a piece of candy or some granulated sugar under their tongue. The sugar will be absorbed into the blood.

If there is no evidence that the victim is diabetic, check skin temperature. When the heat balancing mechanism of the body is disrupted, there is no sweating and the body is too hot. The temperature must be reduced quickly to avoid permanent brain damage.

Always stay with the victim to see that he continues to breathe, and be ready to give CPR whenever needed.

Other causes of unconsciousness are not quite as urgent. We have already covered all the conditions where seconds count, and the ambulance is coming.

Some other causes of unconsciousness are discussed under the proper headings.

Choking

This is commonly caused by a big chunk of food, but it could be a marble or other toy. Sometimes the victim can get it out himself while he breathes around it.

YOUR GOALS ARE:

1. DECIDE WHETHER THE BLOCKAGE IS COMPLETE OR PARTIAL.

2. IF PARTIAL, DO NO HARM BUT WATCH FOR IT TO BECOME COMPLETE.

3. IF COMPLETE, GET AIR INTO THE VICTIM SOMEHOW.

So long as the victim can talk or make any noise, air is moving from the lungs and you must not slap his back or you may actually cause the blockage to move down and block the airway completely. In this case, just encourage the victim who is probably very scared.

If the blockage is complete (the victim cannot make any noise) you try to "blow" the chunk out by forcing air out of the lungs, pretty similar to a pea shooter. To force the air out, use 4 back slaps, then 4 abdominal thrusts.

The squeezed abdomen bulges the muscle between the abdomen and chest (diaphragm) and causes air to be forced out of the chest.

The abdominal thrust could be dangerous to a pregnant woman or impossible in a very fat person, so you would then use the chest thrust. The same thing happens inside.

If the victim's airway does not clear before he falls unconscious, you have to try to get air in before he dies. So try to give a breath. You might actually blow the chunk down further, but sometimes this might open up one lung for the victim to use.

If no air goes in even then, you have to keep up the sequence of 4 back blows, then 4 abdominal thrusts, then try to give a breath.

There is no value to any other first aid, even if the heart stops, until you clear the victim's airway and he gets some breaths.

The first step in any emergency is always the airway. Do not move on until that is okay.

Insulin Reaction

There are two situations which may cause unconsciousness in a diabetic. One is called diabetic coma. It happens when the sugar level in the victim's blood gets very high. This is caused by not having enough insulin in the body.

The other situation is the opposite—there is too much insulin in the body, and the sugar level in the blood is very low. This is an insulin reaction.

Of the two situations, the more dangerous is insulin reaction because the brain suffers permanent damage if the sugar level in the blood is low for very long.

So when you see a diabetic who is unconscious, since it is difficult to tell diabetic coma from an insulin reaction, you treat for the insulin reaction.

YOUR GOAL IS:

TO INCREASE THE AMOUNT OF SUGAR IN THE BLOOD STREAM.

Increasing the amount of sugar in the blood (which carries it to the brain) can lead rapidly to improvements and save the victim from brain damage or death.

On the other hand, a little extra sugar in diabetic coma seldom causes any increased damage.

As always, if the victim is not breathing, and has no pulse, CPR is needed immediately.

Heatstroke

Occasionally the part of the brain that controls body temperature will fail and heatstroke can result. This occurs when a person is in a warm, humid environment.

The skin does not sweat as the temperature climbs higher, blood vessels in the skin swell to give off heat causing the skin to look red. But still there is no sweat, so the temperature can get very high.

Permanent brain damage can result when the temperature gets too high and stays there.

YOUR GOAL IS:

TO LOWER THE BODY TEMPERATURE FAST.

The best way is in a shower or tub of water, but cold, wet towels will do. Just do not waste time, and do not leave the victim until the temperature is down to a safe level.

Chemical In Eye

Some chemicals could cause permanent scars and damage to the eyeball, leading to blindness.

YOUR GOAL IS:

TO REMOVE ALL THE CHEMICALS AND DO IT QUICKLY.

Do not waste time, start rinsing immediately before damage is done. But remember you must rinse the eyeball itself, not the outside of the eyelids.

The victim may have pain and may not want to open his eye, but he must or the chemical will continue to burn.

In order to get all the chemical out, rinse for a full 15 minutes.

Even if the victim says he feels okay, he must be checked by a doctor. The next problem is scarring of the eye after the burn, and the doctor needs to examine the eye and treat accordingly.

Minutes Count

Auto Accident

This is a complicated emergency situation where more than one victim may be involved; where each victim may have more than one injury, and where working conditions are often difficult.

YOUR GOALS ARE:

1. DECIDE WHO NEEDS THE MOST ATTENTION.

2. KEEP OXYGEN FLOWING TO THE BRAIN.

3. STOP THE BLOOD LOSS.

4. PREVENT DAMAGE TO THE SPINAL CORD.

5. DECREASE PAIN.

Be careful you do not become a victim yourself at an accident scene. Take as much time as necessary to be sure the scene is safe. If a wrecked car is still running, it could cause an explosion. Turn off the ignition.

If there is more than one victim, you need to decide who to treat. Therefore, look at everyone quickly and ignore those who are already dead and those who are not injured. Then take care of victims in sequence from the most important things to the least important ones.

a. Unconscious? Be sure they are breathing and the heart is beating. If not, begin CPR.
b. Bad airway problems? Correct it if you can—if not, (as with a severe chest injury causing blue skin and gasping), get victim to a doctor fast.
c. Breathing problems? In an accident, chest injury is the likely culprit. Each kind of chest injury needs a different kind of treatment.
d. Circulation decreased? Could be due to blood loss. Stop the bleeding and treat for shock.

A great danger in auto accidents is internal bleeding which cannot be stopped by any first aid techniques. All you can do is treat for shock and be sure the victim does not move around—lying still may slow the bleeding a little.

After the life-threatening conditions are taken care of, check for spinal injuries. These are frequent in accident cases and if the first-aider makes a mistake with a spinal injury victim, that victim could be paralyzed for life. No doctors can correct the damage afterward. So be very careful if a back injury is possible.

Broken back or neck bones can cut the spinal cord if the victim is twisted, turned, or bent the wrong way. Do not move the victim if you even suspect such an injury.

The obvious exception is when there is immediate danger of death from the car sinking in water, or fire approaching, or if the pulse has stopped. Then you choose life over possible paralysis (a difficult decision).

Broken bones can be very painful, but do not often do permanent damage. You can reduce the pain by keeping the broken bone from moving. To do that, be sure that both the joint above and the joint below the break cannot move.

Do not bother with broken bones until you have reached the first 4 goals for every victim.

Bleeding

The risk in heavy bleeding is that the circulation will decrease to the point that not enough oxygen (which is carried in the blood) will reach the brain.

YOUR GOAL IS:

TO STOP THE BLOOD LOSS.

In most cases, bleeding can be stopped by direct pressure over the wound. Put on plenty of bandage material to soak up the blood, and apply pressure on top.

Do not take off soaked bandages or "take a peek" to see what is happening to the wound as this can break the clots which have formed and slow the bleeding.

If the wound is in an arm or leg, raising it above the heart will help the blood flow back toward the body and slow down the bleeding. Then keeping the wounded arm or leg still will slow the bleeding further and prevent breakage of blood clots.

Some antiseptics can damage healthy tissue—you do not need to worry about infection. Your job is to stop the bleeding.

Sometimes you need to shut off the blood supply to stop the bleeding. That is what happens when you push on a pressure point. But this can be dangerous since all the muscles and skin beyond the pressure point need blood. You could cause permanent damage to a limb by using a pressure point, but you do it to save a life. To minimize the risk of damage, let up on the pressure point when the bleeding stops—push on it if the bleeding starts again. Keep this up and the bleeding will usually stop.

Very rarely, neither direct pressure nor pressure points will stop the bleeding, then you may need to use a tourniquet to save the victim from bleeding to death. But tourniquets are very dangerous and can cause gangrene and loss of an arm or leg. So they are really only safe to use in case of an amputation where part of a limb is already lost, or when shock occurs and the bleeding has not been stopped by other means.

Do not loosen or remove a tourniquet if

you take the drastic step to put one on—poisons from the crushed tissue under it can return to the body and cause shock.

If a lot of blood has been lost, the victim should be treated for shock. Your goal here is to keep blood flowing to the brain. Elevating the legs helps blood drain back to the body and brain. In case of a head injury, however, you want to avoid increasing the pressure and swelling in the brain so do not elevate the legs.

Amputation

As with any kind of heavy bleeding, the risk of an amputation is bleeding to death. Blood carries oxygen to the brain, and if you lose too much blood, the circulation could slow down so that the brain would not get enough oxygen to live.

YOUR GOAL IS:

TO STOP THE BLOOD LOSS.

Direct pressure over the wound will usually be enough to stop the blood loss. Just be sure to use enough bandage material.

Do not take off the bandages, even if they are soaked because that can break up blood clots that have slowed down the bleeding. Peeking underneath to see how things are doing will only cause the bleeding to start again.

Antiseptics may destroy normal tissue and make things worse. Let the doctors worry about preventing infection later, your job is just to stop the bleeding.

Holding the arm or leg higher than the heart will help the blood to drain back toward the body and slow down the amount of blood lost.

If the pressure and elevation do not

stop the bleeding, you need to block the artery that pumps blood to the limb. This is dangerous since the limb needs that blood to live but the victim might be in danger of bleeding to death if you cannot stop the bleeding any other way. When you press on a pressure point, you stop the pulse. So let go as soon as the bleeding stops. But if bleeding starts again, use the pressure point again.

If signs of shock should appear while the victim is still bleeding, you cannot afford to allow any more blood loss. Stop the bleeding immediately, using a tourniquet if necessary. The body can no longer compensate for the blood loss at this point. The brain is already short of blood and oxygen when shock is obvious.

cause gangrene and the loss of a limb. In the case of an amputation, however, part of the limb has already been lost.

Do not loosen or remove a tourniquet once applied. This can release poisonous chemicals into the body and cause shock.

A tourniquet is the last step to control bleeding. Always use direct pressure and, if necessary, pressure points first.

If a lot of blood was lost, treat the victim for shock. Your goal here is to keep blood flowing to the brain. Elevating the legs helps blood drain back to the body and brain.

Once in a while, an amputated part can be used by the doctors, but putting it in liquid can ruin it. Just wrap it up and keep it clean and cold. A plastic bag will keep it dry.

Shock

There are several different kinds of shock, but the one we are concerned with here is blood loss (hemorrhagic) shock.

When there has been a lot of bleeding from wounds or internal bleeding or fluid loss in burns, the blood pressure goes down, just like the pressure in a garden hose goes down if you punch a hole in it. Then what happens is:

1. The brain gets "starved" for blood (and oxygen).
2. The brain tells you to drink (you get thirsty).
3. The brain gets groggy (you get drowsy and restless).
4. The brain tells you to breathe more oxygen (breathing rapid).
5. The heart beats faster to keep the pressure up (pulse gets fast).
6. The blood vessels narrow to save blood for the brain (skin gets pale, cool).

The great danger here is brain damage or death because the brain cannot get enough oxygen.

YOUR GOAL IS:

TO KEEP AS MUCH BLOOD AS POSSIBLE FLOWING TO THE BRAIN (TO SUPPLY OXYGEN).

The best treatment, of course, is to give oxygen and blood transfusions (or at least, intravenous solutions) to raise the oxygen level and blood pressure. But you cannot do that, so you need to stop further blood loss (if possible), and drain blood from the legs toward the brain.

Gravity drains blood away from the brain when the victim is standing or sitting, so lay him down and raise the legs, then gravity will pull blood toward the brain. But, if you suspect a head injury, you want to avoid increasing the pressure and swelling in the brain, so lay the victim flat. Also, moving broken legs around will only increase damage and bleeding. By keeping the victim still, any internal bleeding may slow down a little.

You can control external bleeding by the usual steps (direct pressure/pressure point/tourniquet). But you must stop it very quickly—go directly to using a tourniquet if bleeding is very heavy. The victim in shock is near death and cannot afford any more blood loss.

The victim is losing body heat, so cover him to protect against this.

Since such victims will often need surgery at the hospital, do not give them anything to eat or drink, especially alcohol which will only worsen the situation.

But, if no help is immediately available, the victim may be able to replace some of the blood fluids he lost by taking small amounts of water with salt. (Remember the brain said he is thirsty). Do not give him large amounts, he might vomit. Give small amounts, but give them often.

Chest Injury

The main problems with chest injuries are: the lungs will not work properly and breathing will be limited, there may be heavy bleeding inside the chest, there is pain from broken ribs.

YOUR GOALS ARE:

1. KEEP OXYGEN FLOWING TO THE LUNGS.

2. KEEP BLOOD FLOWING TO THE BRAIN.

3. DECREASE PAIN.

When the chest is injured, the windpipe, throat or face may also be injured.

Check the airway and remove possible blockages like pieces of bone.

Then check the breathing. If there is no breathing, artificial respiration is needed before any further treatment.

Even if artificial respiration is not needed, limitation in breathing is still the major danger in chest injuries. You need to examine for and treat injuries from the most dangerous to the least.

When air pressure is building up in one side of the chest, the heart and lungs may get squeezed to the point that the oxygen supply to the entire body is cut off. The victim will turn blue, appear very sick, and be gasping for breath.

At the first signs of this, rush the victim to a hospital, he could die soon and no first aid treatment will help.

A "sucking chest wound" is a hole in the chest wall where air can rush in and collapse the lung. Stop up the hole with any air-tight bandage, and the lung should not collapse further. Sudden worsening might mean air pressure is building up (as described above) and this pressure can be relieved by opening the hole when the victim breathes out.

When many ribs are broken, a certain portion of the chest may not move normally like the rest of the chest. It goes in when the victim inhales and bulges out when the victim exhales. Because of this, the lungs are not as well filled with air as usual, but simply supporting the "flail segment" will correct a lot of that. Laying the victim down on the injured side will support the segment nicely.

There might be bleeding inside where you cannot see it and cannot control it. So examine and treat for shock, as you would for internal bleeding in the abdomen.

Sometimes removing an object stuck in the chest will cause more bleeding into the chest than if you leave it there. So just try to keep it steady so it will not jiggle around and do more damage.

A broken rib is usually fairly easy to determine. It is no great hazard to the victim if it does not damage other tissue, but it makes breathing painful. Splinting the rib with a strap around the chest eases the pain.

Spinal Injury

Sometimes in an accident someone will break or cause a shifting of one or several of the bones in the spine (vertebrae). This is painful, but seldom causes permanent problems unless the broken (or shifted) vertebrae damage the spinal cord which runs inside the vertebra bones.

YOUR GOAL IS:

TO PREVENT DAMAGE TO THE SPINAL CORD BY PREVENTING MOVEMENT OF THE BROKEN OR SHIFTED VERTEBRAE

This is one of the most important things a first-aider can do. Too often people think they are helping by pulling a victim from a wrecked car or by picking up a victim and carrying him somewhere else. If the spinal cord is damaged during these twisting, bending movements, it may never be repaired. The victim could spend the rest of his life paralyzed.

In the case of an accident where the victim is unconscious, assume he has spinal injuries and treat him that way. This is especially true if there is any evidence of injury to the face or head.

If the victim is awake, ask him if he has neck or back pain. If he is too dazed to answer clearly, treat him for spinal injuries. Tell him to stay still wherever he is.

Of course, the first step (as always) is

to be sure the airway is all right. If you need to open the airway, do so without bending the neck any more than is absolutely necessary. Do not lift the neck and push back the forehead as usual. Keep the neck still and lift the jaw, or pull it forward from the angles of the jaw. You can even give breaths using this technique (if necessary).

Obviously, if it is a choice of possible death or possible spinal cord injury, you do what is necessary to save a life. It can be a difficult decision.

If there is no open airway and no breathing and the jaw lift techniques above do not work, do what is necessary to open the airway and give breaths.

If there is no pulse, CPR is needed and the victim must be lying down on a solid surface to do it. So you might have to move the victim.

Try to keep the neck and back from moving too much. If the victim is in a car which is sinking in water or a fire is starting, you have to move the victim.

To prevent any accidental spinal cord damage while you are waiting for the ambulance, keep the neck stable by holding the head of a sitting victim, or immobilizing the head, neck and spine of a victim lying down.

This will keep the spinal bones (vertebrae) in line so the spinal cord should not be kinked.

Maintain this immobilization until the ambulance crew has attached necessary splints and they say it is okay to let go.

Head Injury

Where there is or has been a head injury, there is danger of: a broken neck, bleeding inside the skull (which could cause death many hours later), and infection in the brain.

YOUR GOALS ARE:

1. PREVENT DAMAGE TO SPINAL CORD.

2. DECREASE BRAIN SWELLING.

3. PREVENT BRAIN INFECTION.

If the victim is unconscious, assume there is a broken neck and treat the victim like a person with a spinal injury. Open the airway while protecting the neck, and clear the airway (the victim may also have injuries to the face).

Keeping the head higher than the chest will prevent increased swelling in the brain, but remember not to bend the possibly broken neck.

If there are open wounds on the head, cover them gently. Pressing on a broken skull could cause pieces of bone to damage the brain.

In victims who were unconscious, but now appear quite normal, there is still the risk of bleeding into the skull which presses on the brain and could cause death. It takes hours or days for this to happen, but the victim must be observed for this possibility to prevent sudden death later.

Do not give the victim anything to eat or drink because he may need to go to surgery. If there is anything in the stomach, the risk of vomiting and pneumonia is much greater.

Do not give him any medicine — this may decrease brain function and make it difficult to decide whether the victim is getting worse from the injury or just being influenced by the medicine.

Heart Attack

The most dangerous period in a heart attack, when most sudden deaths occur, is during the **first two hours** after the pain starts. At any moment, the victim's heart could suddenly stop. Only if CPR (artificial breathing and external compressions) is started immediately can the victim be saved from death.

But if CPR is started immediately, and is done well, without any interruptions, chances for survival are much better.

YOUR GOALS ARE:

1. RECOGNIZE HEART ATTACK.

2. BRING MEDICAL CARE TO THE VICTIM IMMEDIATELY.

3. BE READY TO TREAT SUDDEN HEART STOPPAGE.

4. IF THE HEART STOPS, KEEP OXYGEN FLOWING TO THE BRAIN.

In a heart attack, there is usually chest pain like "heavy pressure" or burning "like indigestion" over the breastbone. The pain may extend to the jaw and arms (usually left arm). Also there may be:

Shortness of breath   Pale or blue skin
Fear   Nausea
Sweating

If the victim is a heart patient and has nitroglycerine pills for heart pain, he may take them as prescribed. But if the pain does not go away after taking the pills, suspect heart attack, not simple heart pain (angina).

Do not drive the victim to the hospital or doctor's office. If you are the victim, do not drive yourself. If the victim's heart suddenly stops in the car, there is no one (and no room) to give CPR and CPR is the only way to save his life.

The ambulance is equipped, staffed, and prepared to deal with this potential problem. Therefore, all possible heart attack victims should go to the hospital in an ambulance.

Do not waste time. The greatest risk is in the first two hours, so the victim should be in the hospital (or at least in an ambulance) during this time. If you "wait to see if it goes away," the victim might die suddenly.

Stay with the victim to watch for sudden heart stoppage. Be prepared to start CPR at any moment before the ambulance comes.

Let the victim tell you how he is comfortable. Often, because of a weak heart, his shortness of breath will get worse lying down.

If the victim is, or suddenly becomes, unconscious, go through the CPR step-by-step sequence and start CPR if necessary. Do not interrupt CPR for more than 5 seconds.

If no one else shows up to call an ambulance and you did not get a chance to call before starting CPR, you may have to leave to call. But continue CPR for at least 5 minutes first, the victim might wake up. Then, make the call quickly, and return to continue CPR.

Many hundreds of heart attack victims' lives have been saved because someone like you gave them the proper care before the ambulance arrived.

Drowning

In rescuing a drowning victim, remember how risky it is to swim out and try to control such a person. Try everything else before swimming out.

Suffocation and low body temperature are the major problems here. But sometimes a neck injury may be suffered if the victim hits bottom with his head.

YOUR GOALS ARE:

1. KEEP OXYGEN FLOWING TO THE BRAIN.

2. PREVENT DAMAGE TO THE SPINAL CORD.

3. MAINTAIN NORMAL BODY TEMPERATURE.

Correct breathing problems as soon as possible. If you are a strong swimmer, you might be able to start artificial respiration before reaching shore, just do not get tired out and risk your own life.

If needed, begin CPR no matter how long the victim has been under water. Some persons have recovered from drowning after being under 20 minutes or more.

Watch for vomiting. You may save a victim with CPR, but if his vomit flows down into his lungs, his chances for survival are small. Do not allow vomit to go down the airway.

In case of possible neck injury, you can get the victim out safely, but you will need help. If there is no one else, you may have no choice but to get the victim ashore (where CPR will work) trying as best you can to keep the neck straight and immobile.

If the victim needs CPR and you suspect neck injury, use the jaw lifting method so you do not bend the neck.

Remember, the drowning victim has suffered severe exposure, so cover him up to get his body temperature increased.

Drug Overdose

The major risks in a case of serious drug overdose are that breathing may stop and that vomit and other fluids may enter the airway and lungs. This progresses as follows:

At first, the victim is awake (but may be groggy). Then the victim becomes unconscious, but is breathing. However, he may not be able to stop vomit or fluids from entering his airway and lungs. Finally, the victim stops breathing.

SO YOUR GOALS IN THE UNCONSCIOUS VICTIM ARE:

1. KEEP OXYGEN FLOWING TO THE BRAIN.

2. PREVENT FLUIDS FROM ENTERING THE AIRWAY.

The victim may stop breathing at any time and need artificial respiration to keep oxygen going to the brain. If you do this well, even a victim who has stopped breathing may eventually wake up with no permanent brain damage.

Keep the victim on his side to allow fluids to drain out, and watch for vomiting.

YOUR GOAL IN THE VICTIM WHO IS AWAKE IS:

TO GET HIM TO THROW UP THE DRUGS IN HIS STOMACH AND THEREFORE, LOWER THE LATER RISK OF A HEAVY OVERDOSE.

It is very helpful to the doctor at the hospital if he knows what kind of pills were taken. So try to find the container or some of the pills.

Poison Swallowed

There are lots of home remedies and first aid tips that have been associated with poisoning over the years.

But today, there are Poison Control Centers and well-informed Emergency Rooms throughout the country, so you do not need to do anything without guidance and help.

YOUR GOALS ARE:

1. FIND OUT EXACTLY WHAT KIND OF POISON WAS SWALLOWED.

2. CALL FOR HELP.

Most Poison Control Centers (P.C.C.'s) have learned that you can treat the majority of poisonings at home, with no need to go to the hospital. Only a small percentage need hospital treatment.

Some "poisons" are not at all dangerous, so there is no reason to panic, all you need to do is call with the information indicated and do what they tell you.

There are some poisons where causing vomiting is the wrong thing to do and could cause more harm. This is the case when acid, lye or other corrosives or petroleum products like lighter fluid are swallowed. Some kinds of vomiting solutions can be hazardous (for instance salt).

Diluting the poison by giving lots of milk or water may make things worse by increasing the speed at which the poison is absorbed.

So remember the golden rule: **FIRST DO**

NO HARM. The only thing you need to do quickly is call.

Convulsions

For some reason, we have grown up afraid of people having seizures, and have thought they should be treated with force during a seizure. Neither idea is correct.

A convulsion can be thought of as a massive electrical stimulation to the brain. It causes all the muscles to get stiff, and the victim will twitch and temporarily stop breathing. There is nothing that first aid can do to stop this process.

YOUR GOAL IS:

TO PROTECT THE VICTIM.

Keep him from falling on sharp objects, from knocking his head on the floor, from striking furniture with his arms and legs. To do this, you will need to move away dangerous objects and perhaps hold him gently.

Do not pin him to the floor so he cannot move at all, some authorities think this might actually make the convulsion worse.

If you can get a soft, firm object between his teeth, you can prevent him from biting his tongue. Swallowing the tongue is not a problem. The victim is not breathing anyway during a seizure. You can do more harm than good if you try to pry the mouth open. Don't bother. Even if he bites his tongue, it will heal. But if you break a tooth, it will not grow back.

After the seizure, the victim will be groggy. Protect him from having fluids run into his airway and lungs by laying him on

his side. For the same reason, avoid giving him food or drink.

After calling an ambulance, stay with him; he might have another seizure.

A high fever in a child can actually cause convulsions (even though the child is not an epileptic). So in this case, first aid can prevent a seizure by lowering the body temperature.

Stroke

A stroke is damage to part of the brain that usually shows itself as a paralyzed arm or leg on one side, numbness of the skin on the same side, or unconsciousness.

Not only is there nothing you can do to cure this situation, there is not much the doctors can do either.

SO YOUR GOAL IS:

TO SUPPORT THE VICTIM UNTIL THE AMBULANCE COMES.

1. Support his airway, breathing, and circulation (as always, the first steps).
2. Support the victim psychologically, often the victim cannot talk because his muscles for talking are paralyzed. But he may be totally aware of what is going on, and probably, he is frightened. Assume he can hear you. Tell him you have called for help and you will stay with him. Do not make any negative comments.

3. Since he may not have the muscle control needed to protect his airway from fluids, vomit and food, lay him on his side to protect the airway and do

not give him anything to eat or drink. He might accidentally get the fluid into his lungs, which could be fatal.

Scratched Eye

The problem with a scratched eyeball is later infection. The eye can heal itself quite well as long as no infection sets in.

YOUR GOAL IS:

TO KEEP IT CLEAN.

1. Wash your hands so you don't put more germs in the eye.
2. Rinse the eye to clean it out.
3. Keep eye closed while going to Emergency Room or doctor's office.

Broken Bones

Broken bones themselves do not cause death. But they can do a lot of damage. The jagged edges cut muscles and veins and cause bleeding in the area of the break. The edge can sometimes cut nerves and major blood vessels. This is particularly true with breaks near joints like the elbow and knee. If the edges poke thru the skin, germs can then enter and cause infection—this is called an open break. A broken bone that does not penetrate the skin is called a closed break. In both cases, the edges grind against each other, causing pain.

YOUR GOALS ARE:

1. STOP THE BLOOD LOSS.

2. KEEP BLOOD FLOWING TO THE BRAIN.

3. PREVENT FURTHER DAMAGE.

4. PREVENT INFECTION.

5. REDUCE PAIN.

The first concerns in a victim with broken bones are not the breaks, but, as always: airway, breathing, pulse, and bleeding.

If it is an open break, control the bleeding with the usual pressure bandage method.

If big bones are broken, or many bones are broken, enough internal bleeding could result to cause shock. Examine and treat for shock to keep oxygen flowing to the brain.

After these concerns are taken care of, examine the victim to see if any nerves have been damaged (the skin below the break will be numb) or any large blood vessels have been cut (there may be no pulse below the break and the skin color will be abnormal).

Immobilizing the broken bone prevents any more damage (the jagged edges of bone are not moving around and slicing the tissue) and reduces pain (the edges are not grinding together).

To do this successfully, you have to keep both the joint above and the joint below from moving.

Do no harm—do not try to straighten broken and displaced bones. That could cause more slicing when you move the bone. Put the splint on the limb in the position you found it. This is especially true for the elbow and knee where nerves and blood vessels are close to the bone.

If it is an open break, cover it. Do not try to clean up the wound, you might get germs and dirt in deeper. An infected bone is very difficult to cure.

Good immobilization will often eliminate the pain completely.

Burns

While some burns can be severe—even fatal, there is seldom any reason to be in a hurry when treating a burn victim.
1. First degree burns can be treated at home.

YOUR GOAL IS:

TO RELIEVE PAIN.

2. Second degree burns mean the skin is damaged to the point of running the risk of infection.

YOUR GOALS ARE:

1. PREVENT INFECTION.

2. RELIEVE PAIN.

The blisters are potential areas for infection to start. If the blisters are not broken, there is no danger of infection. If they are, the tissue underneath is very susceptible to infection which could lead to severe scars later. Butter and ointments can carry germs and cause infection—don't use them. Freshly ironed cloths should be nearly sterile and will not increase the risk of infection while you treat the pain with cold water.

3. Third degree burns mean extensive damage to the skin and other tissue including blood vessels (thus white skin), and nerves (so no pain in a burn is worse than pain).

YOUR GOALS ARE:

1. KEEP OXYGEN FLOWING TO THE BRAIN.

2. PREVENT INFECTION.

3. REDUCE SWELLING.

If the face is burned, or the hairs in the nose are singed, or the mouth cavity is black, or the victim has a deep cough, there is a great risk that the airway and lungs could be burned.

A burned airway may swell shut; check it, and keep the airway open.

Burned lungs collect fluid, causing shortness of breath. Breathing will usually be easier if the victim is sitting up.

There can be a lot of fluid lost from the blood stream when a victim is badly burned. So even though there is no bleeding, the victim may be in shock. Treat him as you would for blood-loss shock because the problems are the same: blood pressure is low; blood supply to the brain is low.

Since vomiting is a risk, most burn victims in shock should have nothing to drink. But, if medical care is not immediately available, you may need to give salt water solution to restore some of the fluids to the victim's blood stream.

The clothes may be burned right into the skin. Removing clothes could cause more damage and open up tissue which could get infected. Of course, any burning or smoldering clothes must be removed or put out immediately.

Elevating burned arms and legs will reduce swelling. Such swelling could itself cause more tissue damage.

It is particularly important that victims get medical attention when burns involve: the face, hands, feet, or the genitals.

Using salt and ice in the water could lower the water temperature enough to actually increase damage to the tissues.

Home First Aid Kit

1. **Syrup of ipecac (***not*** the fluid extract) 1 ounce for each member of family**

2. **Epsom salts**

3. **Roll of 1 inch adhesive tape (1)**

4. **Sterile bandages 4 inch by 4 inch (12)**
   3 inch by 3 inch (12)
   2 inch by 2 inch (12)

5. **Sterile vaseline gauze**

6. **Elastic bandages 2½ inch**
   4 inch

7. **Hydrogen peroxide**

8. **Scissors**

9. **Tweezers**

10. **Insect sting kit (if someone in house is allergic)**

11. **Aspirin (child-proof cap if children in house)**

12. **Children's aspirin (child-proof cap)**

13. **Thermometer**

14. **Cotton-tipped swabs**

15. **Triangle bandage (1)**

16. **Anesthetic ointment**

17. **Antibiotic ointment**

18. **Gauze bandage rolls 1 inch wide**
    4 inches wide

19. **Adhesive bandages, assorted**

Index

Many emergency conditions will be found under several different headings in the index, and will refer you to the proper page. For example: "cuts", "knife wound", "laceration", and "wound" will all give you the page for "bleeding".

Index